THE
MIND OF THE
ISLAMIC
STATE

ISIS AND THE IDEOLOGY
OF THE CALIPHATE

ROBERT MANNE

Prometheus Books

59 John Glenn Drive
Amherst, New York 14228

Originally published by Redback Quarterly,
an imprint of Schwartz Publishing Pty Ltd
Level 1, 221 Drummond Street
Carlton VIC 3053, Australia
Copyright © 2016 Robert Manne
Robert Manne asserts his right to be known as the author of this work.
Published by arrangement with Black Inc.

Cover image © Shutterstock
Cover design © Prometheus Books

Inquiries should be addressed to
Prometheus Books
59 John Glenn Drive
Amherst, New York 14228
VOICE: 716–691–0133
FAX: 716–691–0137
WWW.PROMETHEUSBOOKS.COM

21 20 19 18 17   5 4 3 2 1

Library of Congress Cataloging-in-Publication Data

Names: Manne, Robert, author.
Title: The mind of the Islamic State : ISIS and the ideology of the caliphate / by Robert Manne.
Description: Amherst, New York : Prometheus Books, 2016. |
    Includes bibliographical references and index.
Identifiers: LCCN 2017010207| ISBN 9781633883710 (pbk.) |
    ISBN 9781633883727 (ebook)
Subjects: LCSH: Jihad. | Salafiyah. | Islamic fundamentalism—Middle East. |
    Terrorism—Religious aspects—Islam. | IS (Organization)—History.
Classification: LCC BP182 .M354 2016 | DDC 320.55/7—dc23
LC record available at https://lccn.loc.gov/2017010207

Printed in the United States of America

CONTENTS

GLOSSARY

al-Malhamah al-Kubra: the final, bloodiest battle of the End of
Days

amir: leader

bay'at: oath of loyalty

bidah: an innovation in Islam

Dajjal: Muslim version of the Antichrist

Dar al-Harb: the Abode of War

da'wah: preaching

fard ayn: individual responsibility

fard kifaya: collective responsibility

fatwa: a ruling on a point of Islamic law

fedayeen: Arab guerillas operating especially against Israel

fiqh: jurisprudence

hadith: an account/report of the doings and sayings of
Muhammad

Hanafi: one of the four schools of thought, within Sunni Islam

hakimiyya: sovereignty; in Qutb's thought, the idea that sovereignty belongs not to the state but to God

hijrah: migration, journeying, pilgrimage

huddud: punishments set out in the Qur'an

imam: Muslim religious leader

Kharijites: a sect in the early history of Islam which regarded all
Muslims who differed from their political-religious point of
view as apostates

jahiliyya: condition of spiritual darkness, pre-Islamic ignorance

jihad: struggle; in jihadist thought, armed struggle

kuffar: infidel

Mahdi: Islamic Messiah

mahram: unmarriageable kinsman

mujahidin: those engaged in jihad

Mushrik: polytheist

Rafida: Shi'a Muslims: rejecters of the first three caliphs

Qur'an: sacred scripture of Islam

sharia: Muslim law

Shi'a and **Sunni**: the two major denominations of Islam, originating in the dispute over who should succeed Muhammad as caliph of the Islamic community

taghut: apostate; usually used by jihadis with reference to supposedly Muslim leaders

takfir: excommunication; also the belief that the fate of heretics and apostates should be death

takfiri: excommunicator

tawatur: test used to authenticate hadith

tawhid: the Oneness of God

ulema: Islamic scholarly community

umma: Islamic nation

wala and bara: love of Muslims and hatred of non-Muslims

CHAPTER 1

THE LANDSCAPE OF
SALAFI JIHADISM

In June 2014 the armed forces of the group that at the time called itself the Islamic State of Iraq and al-Sham (ISIS or ISIL)[1] seized Mosul, the second or third most populous city of Iraq. The United States had invested, or perhaps wasted, according to one estimate $25 billion on the Iraqi Army, which now fled in fear.[2] Already ISIS had dissolved the border that divided Iraq and Syria since the end of World War I, which it derisively described as the fruit of the Anglo–French "Sykes–Picot" conspiracy. Shortly after, ISIS shortened its name to the Islamic State and declared that the centuries-old caliphate abolished in 1924 by the Turkish president Kemal Atatürk was now reborn. The caliph was the former head of ISIS, Abu Bakr al-Baghdadi. According to the Islamic State, it was to Baghdadi that the more than one and a half billion Muslims living in every continent across the globe now owed allegiance.

ISIS had been seizing territory in Iraq and Syria during the past two years or more. After Mosul fell, the Islamic State was the size of Belgium. And yet it is also true that until that moment, apart from a handful of scholars and a small number of military strategists and intelligence officers, the advance of ISIS had scarcely been given a second thought in the United States. In early January 2014, the editor of the *New Yorker*, David

Remnick, conducted a wide-ranging foreign policy interview with President Barack Obama. A few days earlier, as Remnick pointed out to Obama, the Sunni city of Fallujah had fallen to ISIS. He challenged Obama: "Even in the period that you've been on vacation in the last couple of weeks, in Iraq, in Syria, of course, in Africa, al-Qaeda is resurgent." Obama replied in a dismissive tone: "Yes, but David, I think the analogy we use around here sometimes, and I think [it] is accurate, is if a JV [junior varsity] team puts on Lakers uniforms, that doesn't make them Kobe Bryant."[3] This comment became notorious. At this time the Obama administration was obviously not concerned with the growing power of ISIS. Neither Remnick nor Obama even seemed to be aware that relations between al-Qaeda and ISIS had broken down. As it happens, in June 2014 I attended a conference in Canberra which was also attended by Kurt Campbell, a former very senior member of the US State Department, recently retired. He seemed no better informed nor less perplexed by the turn of events in Iraq than I was.

Following the fall of Mosul, Western indifference to the rise of ISIS, now the Islamic State, quickly evaporated. As speculation about the security of even Baghdad mounted, the world learned of the many dark and barbarous deeds—the public beheadings of Western hostages; the massacres of captured enemy troops, of Shi'a and Alawite "heretical" Muslims, and of the Druze and Yazidis, all with an openly admitted genocidal purpose; the creation of markets in women for the purpose of sexual slavery; the stoning to death of adulterous wives; the restoration of punishment by crucifixion; the burnings, in one famous case of a captured and caged Jordanian pilot; the killing of homosexuals, thrown from the roof of a town's tallest building. All of these deaths were public. Many became known to the world through widely disseminated high-quality videos and online magazines.

Although I had once read widely about the United States–led March 2003 invasion of Iraq and its catastrophic aftermath, it was only after the fall of Mosul, as information about the crimes of the Islamic State mounted, that I began to study the worldview, or ideology, of its leaders.[4] I did so for a personal reason. Like all Jews of my generation, I grew up under the shadow of the Holocaust. As an undergraduate I had been invited to review Norman Cohn's *Warrant for Genocide,* a history of *The Protocols of the Elders of Zion,* a supposedly authentic document that purported to reveal the secret Jewish war plan for world domination. Cohn outlined the way in which *The Protocols,* which had in fact been forged by the prewar tsarist secret service, influenced the anti-Semitic mind-set of very many Westerners during the interwar period. More importantly, he revealed the way in which it provided Adolf Hitler and the Nazi leadership with a high-level politico-moral justification for the planned extermination of the Jewish people, with what Cohn called their "warrant for genocide." Of course, *The Protocols* was not the only intellectual source of Nazi anti-Semitism. Cohn's book led me to other historical studies of pre-Nazi German anti-Semitism that were influential in the 1960s, like George Mosse's investigation of *volkisch* thought, *The Crisis of German Ideology,* and Fritz Stern's *The Politics of Cultural Despair.* While it was obvious that anti-Semitism was not the principal reason for the Nazis' rise to power, it was equally obvious, or so it seemed to me, that without an understanding of the stream of thought to which they were heirs (which has been characterized as exterminatory anti-Semitism), the Nazi state's decision to attempt to remove the Jewish people in its entirety from the face of the earth would remain obscure.

Ever since the 1960s, I have believed that there is nothing more dangerous in human affairs than systems of belief—worldviews, or ideologies—capable of convincing those followers of these ideas who have taken control of states or quasi-states of the nobility of mass murder and of other savage acts. Nothing I have read since then about other murderous regimes of the twentieth century—Stalin's Soviet Union, Mao's China, Pol Pot's Cambodia, General Suharto's Indonesia in the second half of the 1960s—has caused me to question this belief. For this reason, once my curiosity about the crimes of the Islamic State had been aroused, I set out to discover whatever I could about the pattern of ideas that have shaped their leaders' thought, or what I call the mind of the Islamic State. This book is the result of that investigation.

During the period of my research, the Islamic State published in several languages, including English, a quarterly online magazine called *Dabiq*. *Dabiq* was clearly written by a number of intellectuals with a grasp of the principal sources of the religion of Islam. Each issue was between sixty and eighty pages, and included a number of well-written articles, sometimes very lengthy. In *Dabiq*, no theme was more important than the Islamic State's desire to destroy those it regarded as its historical and current enemies—especially the Shi'a Muslims; the *Rafida*; their Syrian cousins, the Alawites or Nusayris; the fallen apostate peoples, the Yazidis and the Druze; the Christian West, the "Crusaders"; and the eternal enemy of the Muslims, the Jews. Despite its intellectual sophistication, each issue of *Dabiq* contained eschatological articles, concerning, for example, the nature of the *Dajjal* (the *Rafida* equivalent of the Antichrist) or the coming battles at the End of Days, from whose proph-esied battleground, the town of Dabiq, the magazine took its name.

The magazine had several regular features. Each issue pro-vided details of the military triumphs of the Islamic State and its affiliates, including both the planned operations and the lone wolf attacks on its Crusader enemies in the West. (It was, however, conspicuously silent about the setbacks.) Each issue contained gruesome photos of the enemies it had dispatched—the beheaded Western or Japanese hostages, the immolated Jordanian pilot, and dozens showing the corpses of the cap-tured enemy troops and of the Shi'as, Alawites, or Yazidis it had slaughtered. Each issue told the story of the noble mujahidin "martyrs," under the rubric "Among the Believers Are Men." In a regular column called "From Our Sisters," questions con-cerning women were discussed—the benefits of polygyny; the merits of sexual slavery; and the mothers' indispensable role in providing a suitable education for the "lion cubs," the next generation of soldiers. One of *Dabiq*'s preoccupations was the horror of life in the infidel (*kuffar*) societies of the West and the religious obligation of Muslims around the world to undertake migration to the Islamic State (*hijrah*) now that the caliphate has been established.

Dabiq was obsessed by the internal micro-politics of the civil war in Syria and especially the Islamic State's enmity with its former Syrian ally there, the al-Nusra Front. It also became obsessed with the weakness and betrayal of the Muslim cause of Ayman al-Zawahiri, the current leader of al-Qaeda. In several issues, *Dabiq* published strange non-Islamic articles by one of its Western hostages, John Cantlie, who, in the sarcastic tone of a contemporary "Lord Haw-Haw," castigated the United States for its cruelty and its folly. *Dabiq* contained a regular feature it called "In the Words of the Enemy." Here, special pleasure was taken in the comments of leading American generals, politicians or journalists expressing anxiety about the growing strength of the Islamic State and the danger it posed.

The pages of *Dabiq* express a remarkably consistent and internally coherent ideology, no less consistent and coherent than the Marxism–Leninism of the Soviet Union during the era of Stalin; more consistent and coherent, in my view, than the ideology of Nazism. As one can assume that *Dabiq* represents the official worldview of the Islamic State, it is surprising how little it has been analyzed by specialist scholars. It has been my primary source for an understanding of the mind of the current leadership of the Islamic State.

Political ideologies take decades to form. The mind of the Islamic State represents the most recent iteration of an ideology that has been developing over the past fifty years. Among scholars there is little disagreement about who have been its most significant contributors. There exists a more or less general consensus that the ideology of the Islamic State is founded upon the prison writings of the revolutionary Egyptian Muslim Brother Sayyid Qutb, in particular some sections of his commentary *In the Shade of the Qur'an*, but most importantly his late visionary work *Milestones*, published in 1964. Qutb argued that the entire world, including the supposedly Muslim states, had fallen into a time of pre-Islamic ignorance, *jahiliyya*, or pagan darkness. He called upon the small number of true

Muslims to form a revolutionary vanguard to restore the light of Islam to the world. Because of his reference to the vanguard, the eminent scholar of radical Islam Gilles Kepel has described *Milestones* as the Islamist version of Lenin's *What Is to Be Done?*[5] This seems to me mistaken. Although *Milestones* played a part in the decision of the Egyptian court to send Qutb to the gallows, unlike Lenin's seminal manifesto, the practical political implications of Qutb's masterwork were ambiguous. Nonetheless, so powerful was Qutb's vision that several scholars have termed the ideology that provided the foundation of the Islamic State "Qutbism."

The first answer to the question about what was to be done by those who hoped to implement Qutb's vision came a decade and a half after the master's death, with *The Neglected Duty*, the underground revolutionary working paper of an Egyptian electrical engineer, Muhammad Abd al-Salam Faraj. Faraj called upon Muslims to fulfill their religious obligation of jihad—which he, like Qutb, interpreted as violent struggle in the service of God—and to lay the foundation of a truly Islamic state. His favored method was assassination of the most important contemporary enemy of the Muslims, the apostate "Pharaoh," a clear reference to the president of Egypt, Anwar Sadat. Faraj regarded the "near enemy," the Egyptian state, as a more strategically significant target than the "far enemy," the Crusader Americans and the Zionist Jews. In 1981 Faraj's group succeeded in its plot to kill Sadat. As a consequence, Faraj's life, like Qutb's, ended on the gallows.[6] His pamphlet nonetheless represented the beginning of a twenty-year era during which Egyptian jihadist revolutionaries, under the spell of Qutb's prison writings, conducted a prolonged, bloody and ultimately unsuccessful revolutionary struggle against the "near enemy"—with plots to assassinate the apostate leaders, the *taghut*; to stage military coups; to incite popular uprisings.

A more influential answer to the question of what was to be done to implement the Qutbist vision was provided shortly after Faraj's death, by the Palestinian Islamic scholar Abdullah Azzam. Following the 1979 Soviet invasion of Afghanistan, Azzam moved to Peshawar and established an office for the organization of Arabs who had journeyed to Afghanistan to support the local jihadi fighters, the mujahidin. In remarkably eloquent speeches, in the articles of his magazine, *Al-Jihad*, and especially in two of his short books, *The Defence of the Muslim Lands* and *Join the Caravan*, Azzam called upon Muslims across the globe to defend their nation, the *umma*, which was now under direct threat. Azzam insisted that defense of the *umma* through jihad, in the face of the infidel invader, was not a collective but an individual duty for each Muslim, as obligatory as one of the five pillars of the faith, like praying or fasting. Azzam was assassinated in 1989; nobody knows for certain by whom. However, by the time of his death, he had convinced a generation of revolutionary Muslims that the Afghan and Arab mujahidin had been responsible, through God's grace and through their glorious martyrs' deaths, for crippling the military might of the Soviet Union in Afghanistan. Moreover, he saw in the triumphant struggles of the mujahidin in Afghanistan a portent of a worldwide Islamic revival—in the *jahili* Muslim lands of the present; in his homeland, Palestine, and all other Muslim lands that had been conquered by the Crusaders; eventually across the entire globe.

In Afghanistan, Azzam had worked for a time with a wealthy

Saudi of Yemeni background, Osama bin Laden. Eventually their ways parted. Having absorbed both Qutb's vision and Azzam's triumphalism and ambition (which he assimilated into his Saudi sensibility), in 1988 bin Laden created in Afghanistan an organization he called al-Qaeda, which was eventually to become the first global army of jihadists.[7] In 1996, upon his return to Afghanistan, bin Laden set his sights on the destruction of the only remaining superpower, the United States. In his view, the United States was under the control of the Jews. It had been responsible for inflicting upon the Muslims the cruelest wound, the creation of a Jewish state at the very heart of the *umma*. It was also the indispensable patron and protector of the *taghut* regimes throughout the supposedly Muslim world. Perhaps worst of all, since 1990, by invitation from the Saudi royal family following Iraq's invasion of Kuwait, the United States had occupied the land of the two holiest cities of Islam, Mecca and Medina. In 1998 al-Qaeda called upon the mujahidin to kill Americans and Jews.[8]

One of the signatories of bin Laden's fatwa was the most influential Egyptian Qutbist revolutionary of the past twenty years, Ayman al-Zawahiri. In mid-2001 Zawahiri led a part of his group, al-Jihad, into al-Qaeda. Their union was consummated with a double conversion. Zawahiri adopted bin Laden's concentration on the far enemy. For his part, bin Laden adopted the tactic that Zawahiri and other Egyptian Islamist revolutionaries had long embraced: suicide bombings, or what the Qutbists now called "martyrdom operations"—a vital tactic in technologically unequal, asymmetrical warfare. The first fruit of their union was 9/11, the attack on the Twin Towers in New York and the Pentagon. By this time, Zawahiri was responsible, most comprehensively in his 2001 memoir, *Knights under the Prophet's Banner*, for systematizing the political ideology founded on the vision of Sayyid Qutb.

The ideology had not yet reached its most recent and perhaps final destination. One consequence of 9/11 was the March 2003 United States–led invasion and occupation of Iraq. As it happened, one leader of the Sunni resistance was a Jordanian revolutionary jihadist, Abu Musab al-Zarqawi, who had established his own training camp in Afghanistan in 1999 at Herat and then, after the American invasion of Afghanistan and attack on the Taliban, had moved to Iraq via Iran in preparation for the generally anticipated American invasion.

Zarqawi was responsible for adding several new elements to the political ideology inspired by Qutb and systematized most recently by Zawahiri. Zarqawi injected into its heart a sectarian and exterminatory hatred of the Shi'a.[9] Drawing upon the strategic theory of Abu Bakr Naji, the author of *The Management of Savagery*, and the theology of a jihadist scholar, Abu Abdullah al-Muhajir, the author of a work most commonly known as *The Jurisprudence of Blood*, Zarqawi extended vastly the purpose, the method, and the permissible scope of killing. He conducted public beheadings of hostages.[10] He greatly expanded the role of suicide bombings, with increasingly callous theological justifications, targeting not only the occupation forces and their Iraqi allies but also innocent Shi'a civilians and politically unfriendly Sunnis, earning for himself the well-deserved title of "the sheikh of the slaughterers." Before Zarqawi, the creation of an Islamic State, and even more the re-establishment of the caliphate, had been distant dreams of the Qutbists. With Zarqawi they became pressing items of a current political agenda. Before Zarqawi, too, the thought of the Qutbists had been largely unaffected by the eschatological or apocalyptic undercurrents of Sunni Islam. Under Zarqawi these began to rise to the surface.

Zarqawi was killed in 2006. Nonetheless, his two successors, Abu Omar al-Baghdadi, who was killed in 2010, and Abu Bakr al-Baghdadi, the first caliph of the Islamic State, embraced fully and even extended the anti-Shi'a sectarianism, the strategic and jurisprudential savagery, the immediate Islamic state-building ambition, and the apocalyptic dimension that Zarqawi had injected into the political ideology that had grown from the vision of Qutb. A supporter of the Islamic State, thought to be the Yemeni journalist Abdulelah Haider Shaye, captured with admirable precision in a single sentence its ideological genealogy: "The Islamic State was drafted by Sayyid Qutb, taught by Abdullah Azzam, globalized by Osama bin Laden, transferred to reality by Abu Musab al-Zarqawi, and implemented by al-Baghdadis: Abu Omar and Abu Bakr."[11]

Ever since 9/11 there has been considerable uncertainty and debate about what this ideology should be called. For some time, hawkish conservatives in the West and even former leftists, like Christopher Hitchens, called the ideology associated with al-Qaeda "Islamo-Fascism."[12] This label was adopted for polemical reasons and was quite misleading. There is little overlap between fascism and the ideology stretching from Qutb to Zarqawi. Take just two examples. Fascism is closely associated with racism. Every follower of Qutb abhors the division of humankind into races, dividing humankind rather into two quite different if no less exclusive or absolutist categories: believers and infidels. Fascists are nothing if not believers in the lawmaking role of the charismatic leader and in the unconstrained sovereignty of the state. Qutb and his followers regard all of these ideas—leader worship, man-made law, and the sovereignty of the state—as anathema. For them, leader worship is a form of idolatry in conflict with the most critical concept of their faith, *tawhid*, the Oneness of God; the sharia is the sole source of legitimate law; and sovereignty belongs not to the state but exclusively to God, an idea captured by one of Qutb's most fundamental concepts: *hakimiyya*. Because the term "fascism" is indelibly associated with the war against Hitler's Germany and Mussolini's Italy, labeling the ideology of al-Qaeda "Islamo-Fascism" bestowed an additional political benefit on those who used the term, providing a blessing not only for the muscular prosecution of the "war on terror" but also for the post-9/11 decision to invade Iraq.

Some have wanted to call the ideology shared by the followers of Qutb over the past fifty years "Qutbism," in much the same way that the followers of Karl Marx have always been called Marxists.[13] The advantage of the label "Qutbism" is that it captures accurately the intellectual origins of the ideology that led to both al-Qaeda and the Islamic State. Its disadvantage is that it altogether neglects the profound changes the ideology has undergone over the past fifty years, changes would render it, in my opinion, both unrecognizable and most likely repugnant to its founding father. During the Soviet era, for good reason, the ideology of the state was called not Marxism but Marxism–Leninism. No one has suggested calling the ideology of the Islamic State Qutbism–Zarqawism or some such equivalent.

Some have suggested that the ideology should be called "Islamic fundamentalism," using the name that has been applied to American Protestant biblical textual literalists in the United States.[14] Apart from the difficulty of shrugging off its Protestant American associations, the term "Islamic fundamentalism" in no way allows for a distinction to be drawn between textually literalist but politically quietist Muslims and the textually literalist but politically revolutionary jihadists.

Frequently the supporters of al-Qaeda and the Islamic State have simply been labeled "Islamists," meaning those who aspire to shape the political order according to the sharia law found in the Qur'an. However, because the term fails to distinguish between those, like the Muslim Brothers in Egypt, who have made their peace with the parliamentary process and have foresworn the use of violence, and those, like the members of al-Qaeda and the Islamic State, who are revolutionary jihadists, the term "Islamism" is almost self-evidently inadequate and misleading. A similar problem arises from the term "radical Islam," which has also been very widely used. One problem here is that it cannot be assumed that in common usage the word "radical" has an exclusively political rather than an additional or alternative theological provenance. Even if this is assumed, there is no reason why the term "radical Islam" might not be equally accurately applied to altogether different contemporary and undeniably radical Islamic political tendencies, like the Sunni political movement, Hamas, or the Shi'a political movement, Hezbollah.

Eventually, a genuinely accurate term was discovered for

the followers of the Qutbist tradition—Salafi jihadism or, less frequently, jihadi Salafism—which both scholars hostile to the ideology and its most enthusiastic supporters generally now embrace. This near-universal acceptance of the term is not difficult to explain. The Salafis are those Muslims who regard the period of the Prophet Muhammad and his companions as history's golden age, which all subsequent generations of Muslims are obliged to learn from and to emulate. They are also textual literalists who regard the Qur'an, the book that Muslims believe God dictated to the Prophet Muhammad, and the stories of the life and sayings of the Prophet that are recorded in the authentic hadiths, as providing, without need for further interpretation or adaptation, the source of all fundamentally important human knowledge. In a seminal article of 2005, Quintan Wiktorowicz divided the Salafis into three basic ideal types— the "purists" who avoided engagement in the political sphere altogether; the "politicos" who were interested in engaging in politics from the sidelines, so as to nudge the world in the direction they considered favorable to Islam; and the jihadis, the believers in the revolutionary transformation of the world through violent means.[15] In essence, those adhering to the ideology stretching from Qutb to the Islamic State belong to Wiktorowicz's third category. They are Salafis, textual literalists who regard the Qur'an and the hadiths as the source of vital knowledge, and who regard the time of Mecca and Medina as a golden age. Equally, they are jihadists who believe there is an inescapable religious obligation to commit one's life to violent struggle for the creation of a truly Islamic world.

There is, however, a complication in the use of the term "Salafi jihadism." The Salafi movement is now so closely connected to Saudi Arabia that it is not unusual for "Salafism" to be used almost interchangeably with "Wahhabism," which was named after the eighteenth-century theological founding father of the Saudi Salafi movement, Muhammad ibn Abd al-Wahhab. Yet the Salafi jihadist movement is by no means an exclusively or even principally Saudi or Wahhabist phenomenon. The origin of the tradition is located, if anywhere, not in Saudi Wahhabism but among those jihadist revolutionaries of a Salafist persuasion, Sayyid Qutb and his followers, who had emerged out of but then passed beyond the movement of the Egyptian Muslim Brothers. Qutbists in political exile from the Egyptian regime and Wahhabis first rubbed shoulders in Saudi Arabia in the late 1960s and the 1970s. From the mid-1980s they fought and talked and argued together in Afghanistan. The Salafi jihadist movement, which originated in Egypt during the late 1960s and the 1970s and expanded during the 1980s in the war against the Soviet Army in Afghanistan, represents the fusion of Salafi-inflected Egyptian revolutionary jihadism and politically awakened Saudi Wahhabism.

One overwhelmingly important problem that must be confronted in any attempt to understand the mind of the Islamic State is the progressive radicalization or brutalization of both the Salafi jihadist ideology and the behavior of its adherents, between its origins in the vision of Sayyid Qutb and its culmination in the present criminality of the followers of Abu Bakr al-Baghdadi. One simple way of demonstrating this cumulative and progressive radicalization and brutalization is to examine whom the central figures in the evolution of the ideology set their sights upon killing.

In his final days, Qutb was prepared to justify violence by his Islamic vanguard if they needed to defend themselves against the repressive acts of the Egyptian state. Faraj and the other revolutionary jihadists of his generation plotted to assassinate the Egyptian president and other leading figures of the apostate and repressive Egyptian state. Azzam called upon all Muslims to engage in defensive war against the Soviet Army and its Afghan communist supporters and, beyond that, against the armed forces of the Zionists and the Crusaders and the supporters of Israel. In addition to the officials of the *taghut* regimes, Faraj's target, and the armed forces or supporters of the enemies occupying Muslim lands, Azzam's target, Osama bin Laden and Ayman al-Zawahiri called upon their supporters to kill, wherever possible, Jewish and American civilians. In the case of the Jews, the prime justification was that they supported Israel, the obscene Zionist state entity that had been established in the heart of the *umma*. In the case of the Americans, the justification was that they had voted for governments that had created Israel; that had committed serial crimes against Muslims, for example, the Palestinian and Iraqi peoples; that had occupied the land of Islam's two holy cities; and that were intent on the domination of the entire Muslim world.

The leaders of al-Qaeda called upon their followers to kill the armed forces and civilian populations of the Zionists and the Crusaders. Zarqawi and his successors, Abu Omar al-Baghdadi and Abu Bakr al-Baghdadi, targeted all Shi'a Muslims, Alawites, Yazidis, Druze, and all of the "apostate" Sunni Muslims who actively opposed the Islamic State. They also targeted those they regarded as serious sinners, like promiscuous women, adulterous wives, homosexual men, consumers of alcohol, drug-takers and so on. The only bridge too far for the murderous inclinations of the Islamic State was the general Sunni population. Early in its history the Islamic State announced that its secret police had uncovered a cell of extremists who wanted to target politically neutral Sunnis on the principle that "those who are not for us are against us." The Islamic State described those who wanted to target politically neutral Sunnis on such grounds as Kharijites, the name of a sect in the early history of Islam which regarded all Muslims who differed in any way from their political-religious point of view as apostates deserving either excommunication or death. Unsurprisingly, Kharijites were added to the list of those whom the Islamic State was determined to kill.[16]

There are two principal ways of explaining the progressive radicalization and brutalization of the ideology and the behavior of the Salafi jihadists. One explanation has been provided by the jihadist but non-Salafi veteran of the Afghan war Mustafa Hamid, in his fascinating conversations with the former Australian intelligence officer and current academic Leah Farrall, in their co-authored book, *The Arabs at War in Afghanistan*. According to Hamid, following the ill-prepared and ill-fated Battle of Jalalabad in 1989, where al-Qaeda led "thousands" of jihadis to their deaths, the political authority of both Osama bin Laden and the soon-to-be-assassinated Abdullah Azzam evaporated for a new generation of even more radical, extreme, and violent Salafi jihadists, who lost interest in the political consequences or the moral meaning of their increasingly devil-may-care beliefs and behavior. Hamid calls this tendency the "School of the Youth," or the "Jalalabad School."[17]

According to this interpretation, one result of the emergence of this school of youthful jihadi revolutionaries was the disastrous trajectory of the Algerian Civil War. By the mid-1990s, under the leadership and inspiration of members of the Jalalabad School, the most radical element among the Algerian Salafi jihadists—the Armed Islamic Group—began a murder campaign that in the end targeted almost the entire civilian Sunni population of Algeria. Its logic was outlined in a communiqué it published in January 1997: "There is no neutrality in the war we are waging. With the exception of those who are with us, all the others are apostates and deserve to die."[18] What Hamid's analysis suggests is that another result of the emergence of the ultra-radical Jalalabad School was the political trajectory taken by Abu Musab al-Zarqawi in post-invasion Iraq. By his ruthless targeting of Shi'a holy sites and the Shi'a civilian population, Zarqawi was in large part responsible for transforming resistance to the American occupation of Iraq into a full-blown Sunni–Shi'a civil war. This, in turn, prepared the way for the creation of the Islamic State.

An alternative explanation for the progressive radicalization and brutalization of Salafi jihadist ideology and behavior is the nature of the original idea. Such an explanation would go something like this. Qutb's vision was of a fallen *jahili* world that could only be redeemed by the commitment of the small Muslim vanguard to the religious obligation of jihad. Without victory in such a struggle and the creation of an Islamic world there was no hope for humankind. Only once in human history had there been an era of light—during the time of the Prophet

Muhammad on the Arabian Peninsula in the seventh century. If an era of light was to be restored, it would have to be modeled on the religious understandings, the legal, political, and ethical principles, and the military ethos of the original seventh-century Islamic state. This vision, such an explanation would continue, was so wildly out of touch with the political, moral, and material circumstances of the late twentieth century, that it was inevitable that all attempts to realize it would fail. Rather, however, than acknowledging that the cause of the failure resided in the impossibility of the original utopian ambition, following each inevitable failure those clinging to the original Qutbist vision could find no other resolution of their dilemma than to resort to increasingly brutal and violent methods of jihad and to increasingly irrational and apocalyptic beliefs.

None of this is meant to suggest that Qutb can somehow be held responsible for the beliefs and behavior of the leaders of the Islamic State. Without Qutb's vision it is difficult to see how the Islamic State would have taken the shape that it did. Yet without the influence of a series of historical events for which Qutb self-evidently bears no responsibility—the impact of the Afghan war; the response of the United States administration to the 9/11 terrorist attack and in particular its decision to invade Iraq; the astonishing incompetence of the American occupation; the viciously sectarian behavior of the Shi'a political leadership during and after the American occupation; the outbreak of civil war in Syria following the Arab Spring—it is difficult to imagine that the Islamic State would have ever come into being. Qutb bears the kind of responsibility for the Islamic State that Karl Marx bears with regard to Stalin's Soviet Union. Just as Marx's thought led to Stalin via the Russian populist

Jacobin Pyotr Tkachev and then Lenin, so did Qutb's thought lead to Zarqawi and the two Baghdadis via Faraj, Azzam, bin Laden, and Zawahiri. Yet just as it is more than doubtful that Marx would have regarded the Stalin monster state with favor, so is it implausible to imagine that Qutb would have approved of the brutal beliefs and actions of the Islamic State or regarded it as the fulfillment of his vision. As will be shown, even some of the most extreme political and theological Salafi jihadists of an earlier generation—like the second-in-command and then leader of al-Qaeda Ayman al-Zawahiri, and one of Zarqawi's mentors, the radical Salafi jihadist theologian Abu Muhammad al-Maqdisi—were disturbed by the behavior and beliefs of Zarqawi and his Islamic State successors.

There is one dimension of the mind of the Islamic State that differentiates it starkly from even the most murderous regimes of the twentieth century. Stalin's Soviet Union and Hitler's Germany made considerable effort to disguise their crimes from the eyes of the world. Because of this, Western communists were able to deny for decades the extent of the death toll in Ukraine and Kazakhstan during the collectivization drive of the early 1930s or the executions and expansion of the gulag archipelago during the Great Terror in the late 1930s. Similarly, because of this, it was only when American and British troops stumbled upon the mountains of corpses in the concentration camps in Germany and Soviet troops reached the extermination centers the Germans had built on Polish soil that the world began to understand the nature of what came to be called the Holocaust, the Nazi ambition to rid the earth of the Jewish people.

By contrast the Islamic State has made a considerable effort to publicize its killings. It has produced and then distributed widely videos and photographs of the hostages its operatives beheaded and of the captured Jordanian pilot it caged and then burned to death.[19] In one issue of *Dabiq* there are photographs of an adulterous woman being stoned to death and of a "sodomite" thrown from the roof of a tall building into a public square packed with apparently admiring onlookers. In almost every issue there are before-and-after photographs of the enemies of the Islamic State its soldiers systematically slaughtered. Some of these are of enemy troops. Others are of enemy peoples—the Shi'as, the Alawites, the Yazidis, and the Druze. In these cases, there is no attempt to disguise the genocidal purpose. In the most important historico-eschatological article of *Dabiq* demonstrating the evil nature of the Shi'as, the *Rafida,* the Islamic State announced its intention with regard to its eternal enemy with these words: "The Rafidah are mushrik [polytheist] apostates who must be killed wherever they are to be found, until no Rafidi walks on the face of the earth."[20]

The international community has had difficulty understanding, at least imaginatively, this dimension of the mind of the Islamic State. When, for example, Iraqi troops liberated Fallujah in June 2016, Western newspapers reported that a mass grave containing several hundred bodies had been uncovered, in a tone that suggested an open question about the existence of the Islamic State's killing fields had now come closer to being resolved.[21] For some reason, Western opinion had not yet grasped that the mass killings of the Islamic State were no secret and that evidence of these killing fields could readily be found in the videos and magazines disseminated widely by its own propaganda department. One of the matters that this book will try to reveal is why, among even the most heinous regimes or movements of recent history, it is only the Islamic State that regarded what the world would come to judge as their darkest deeds not with shame but with pride.

CHAPTER 2

MILESTONES—
SAYYID QUTB

Sayyid Qutb was a distinguished and prolific Egyptian poet, essayist, literary critic, and educational civil servant who, around the age of forty, turned from secularism toward Islam and the study of the Qur'an.[1] Qutb's political and religious essays were by now sufficiently radical to disturb the Egyptian royal palace. According to one account, one of his superiors in the Ministry of Education suggested that his outlook might moderate if he embarked on a study tour in the United States. Qutb's American experience did not have the desired effect. He was appalled by the racism, sexual freedom, and materialism he encountered.[2]

By the time Qutb returned to Egypt one of his most popular and important books, *Social Justice in Islam*, had been published. A number of younger members of the Muslim Brotherhood, the mass Islamic movement established by Hassan al-Banna in 1928, sought him out. Although he had formerly been hostile to the Brotherhood, in the early 1950s Qutb "gravitated" into their orbit, as his biographer, John Calvert, puts it. In 1953 Qutb was elected to the Brotherhood's Guidance Office and appointed as the leader of its influential Propagation of the Call Department. By this time the monarchy had been overthrown, in what was known as the Free Officers Revolution.

Initially, Qutb enjoyed close relations with the new leader, Gamal Abdel Nasser. These relations quickly broke down. Following an assassination attempt on the president in October 1954, Qutb was arrested along with a thousand members of the Brotherhood. In July 1955 he received a fifteen-year sentence. Because of ill health, he spent most of the rest of his life in the infirmary of Tora, a Cairo prison. In 1957 he witnessed and was appalled by the slaughter of twenty-one Brothers who, fearing for their lives, had refused to leave their cells for a work detail.[3]

By the time Qutb entered prison, he had begun what most critics regard as his masterwork, *In the Shade of the Qur'an*. He was allowed to continue writing and publishing it during his time in prison. Eventually there were thirty volumes. Unlike most traditional Qur'anic commentaries, which are fustily textual, it is a literary work of considerable power and beauty. As Qutb explained, "I did not want to drown myself in matters of language, diction or *fiqh* ('jurisprudence') that would shield the Qur'an from my spirit, and my spirit from the Qur'an."[4] According to Calvert, Qutb's "daily immersion" in the Qur'an brought him "inner happiness."[5] In the early 1960s, while still in prison, Qutb acted as spiritual and political adviser to a revolutionary group of young Muslim Brothers meeting secretly in the Cairo apartment of one of its female leaders, Zaynab al-Ghazali. At this time Qutb was composing a political manifesto, *Milestones*. Qutb's sister delivered its pages regularly to the Ghazali group. In 1964 the text of *Milestones* was completed. Before it was banned, within six months it went through five editions.[6]

In the same year, following a heart attack and after the intervention of the Iraqi president, Qutb was released from prison.

He was now able to meet in person with the Ghazali group. Qutb discovered that they were planning an armed action to avenge the deaths of those Brothers whose lives were taken in the regime crackdown of 1954. Qutb urged caution, although he also argued that a defensive armed response would be justified in the face of repressive state action. The Ghazali plot was uncovered. In part because of his connection to the group and in part because of *Milestones*, Qutb was re-arrested. In August 1966 he was condemned to death. A story circulated, which Calvert thinks possibly apocryphal, that on the scaffold Qutb received "from a high ranking officer" a presidential offer of clemency in return for "an admission of guilt and an apology." "Sayyid looked up with his clear eyes. A smile, which one cannot describe, appeared on his face. He told the officer in a surprisingly calm tone: 'Never! I would not exchange this temporary life [for] a life which will never disappear.'"[7] The present head of al-Qaeda, Ayman al-Zawahiri, from a prosperous and highly educated Egyptian family, was fifteen at the time. Shortly after learning, to his grief and horror, of Qutb's execution, he committed his life to the Islamist revolutionary underground.[8] With Qutb's death, the movement that would become known as Salafi jihadism had its first and still, perhaps, most important martyr.

There is almost universal agreement among scholars that the publication of *Milestones* marks the intellectual origin of the Salafi jihadist movement and that it provided the movement with its seminal text. As such, *Milestones* is one of the most consequential ideological interventions of the twentieth century. If the genealogy of Salafi jihadism and the mind of the Islamic State are to be understood, acquaintance with both its argument and its spirit is vital.

The argument of *Milestones* is framed by two concepts—*jahiliyya* and *hakimiyya*—that Qutb encountered through the writing of a contemporary Islamist theoretician of equal stature, the Indian then Pakistani Abul A'la Maududi.[9] The term *jahiliyya*, which is usually translated as "ignorance," and which appears in the Qur'an on four occasions, has three rather different meanings. In its simplest and most common meaning, *jahiliyya* represents a historical era, the pagan period in the Arabian Peninsula before the arrival of the religion brought by Muhammad. *Jahiliyya*, however, has a secondary cultural meaning, roughly equivalent to the English word "barbarism." In Qutb's usage *jahiliyya* absorbs but goes beyond both ignorance and barbarism. For him, *jahiliyya* is the terrible condition of a world in the state of spiritual darkness, unenlightened by humankind's submission to God.[10]

In this way, the idea of *jahiliyya* is linked in Qutb's thought to *hakimiyya*, a word that he discovered in Maududi and that does not appear in the Qur'an. *Hakimiyya* has a straightforward meaning—"sovereignty." It is used by Qutb, as it was by Maududi, to suggest that in the world there are only two possibilities: either God's sovereignty or Man's. In those times or places where God's sovereignty is denied, the condition of spiritual darkness, *jahiliyya*, reigns. The terrifying thought, without which Qutb by the time of the composition of *Milestones* cannot be understood, is that, in his view, the entire world had fallen into the condition of *jahiliyya*. In the very first line of *Milestones* he tells us that the threat of nuclear annihilation hanging over our heads is a symptom, not a cause; that humankind now lives in a world without values that can provide it with guidance or that might "justify its existence."[11]

Where can hope be found? Qutb tells us that he has written *Milestones* for those he calls the Islamic "vanguard."[12] The salvation of humankind from the enveloping darkness of *jahiliyya* now rests upon them. What are they to do? Qutb regards the present age as closely resembling the time when Muhammad in Mecca began spreading the word of God to the generation of his companions, a generation without equal in history.[13] Muhammad might have built an Islamic community on the basis of "nationalism," of Arab resentment at the arrogant behavior of the Romans and the Persians; he might have built it on the basis of the "class envy" of the poor; he might have built it on the basis of a program of "moral reform," fighting alcohol, gambling, and fornication—but, according to Qutb, he chose none of these ways.[14]

Rather, Muhammad created in Mecca a community in whose hearts the simple message of the faith—"there is no deity but God, and the Prophet is His Messenger"—has penetrated to the depths. This is what Qutb now calls upon the vanguard to do. He tells them that the Qur'an is the only pure spring from which they can drink.[15] He advises them that they will need to maintain a spiritual separation from the *jahili* society in which they live.[16] He warns them that the task of creating a community of the faithful will require "patience."[17] There is even a suggestion that it might take them as long as the thirteen years it took Muhammad to create the community of the first generation of Muslims. Nor will it arise from theology or theory, but "organically" and as a "living reality" that penetrates "people's hearts."[18] The inspiration can come from a single individual. Three Muslims are enough to create a community. The three will become ten, the ten a hundred, the hundred a thousand, the thousand twelve thousand.[19] During this time, he advises, the vanguard must spread God's word "boldly, clearly, forcefully, without hesitation or doubt," shrugging off the ridicule, the hatred, and the persecution that they will experience.[20] They must endure all of this because of a love even for those who torture them.

Eventually, as it did with Muhammad in Medina, the time will come to fight, to wage jihad. Within Islam there is disagreement about the meaning of this term. Some Muslims turn to the hadith that claims the highest form of jihad is the struggle for the purification of the individual soul. Others, including the Salafi jihadists, who generally dismiss the hadith about the highest jihad as inauthentic, regard jihad as violent struggle in the service of God. Qutb is firmly on the side of violence. It is true that in one passage of *Milestones* Qutb does write about the jihad of the soul—the Muslim's inner struggle "against his own desires and ambitions, his personal interests and inclinations"—but in this case individual jihad combating ego is in preparation for war. "Before a Muslim steps into the battlefield, he has already fought a great battle within himself against Satan."[21] Indeed, in *The Shade of the Qur'an* he argues that participation in violent jihad provides the most perfect circumstance for the purification of the soul.[22] According to Qutb, it is foolish to believe that Islam will conquer the world of *jahiliyya* simply by preaching. If that had been the case during the time of the Prophet, "the task of establishing God's religion in the world would have been very easy."[23] Violent struggle for the faith is an act of highest compassion. "If freedom of man on earth" is to be achieved, if the sovereignty of God is to triumph over the sovereignty of Man, then not only preaching but also violent jihad is required. Violent jihad is so fundamental to the mission of Islam, and the threat of *jahiliyya* so ever-present that it will have to be waged until the Day of Judgment has arrived.

Qutb is aware of objections, both internal and external, to Islam, to the idea of violent jihad. One rests on a passage in the Qur'an—"There is no compulsion in religion"—where imposing religion by force is expressly forbidden. Qutb of course accepts this. The purpose of violent jihad, he argues, is not to impose Islam by force but rather to "destroy ... the wall between Islam and individual human beings so that it may address their hearts and minds." It is this wall that "prevents people from reforming their ideas and beliefs," forcing them to follow "their erroneous ways and ... serve human lords instead of the Lord Almighty." There is no connection whatever between compelling belief by force and striving to make "a system of life dominant in the world." The Western scholars, the group whom Qutb calls the orientalists, who claim that Islam imposes religion "by the sword," are guilty of "a vicious lie." Unfortunately, many Muslim scholars have "capitulated to this slander." Because it is "God's religion," "Islam has the right to destroy all obstacles in the form of institutions and traditions which limit man's freedom of choice." Indeed, it has more than a right. "The duty of Islam [is] to annihilate all such systems. ... They are obstacles in the way of human freedom."[24] Rousseau believed people had to be forced to be free. Qutb believes that armed force is needed to give people the freedom to choose Islam, which is the only freedom humans can know.

Qutb is equally contemptuous of another idea that is commonly propagated by the orientalists and that even Islamic scholars now commonly embrace, namely that the only permissible kind of violent jihad is the one conducted in defense of Muslim territory. Of course, he argues, it is true that Islamic territory must be defended when under attack. But the mission of Islam is not the defense of pieces of land. Indeed, the only land that is valuable is where Islam has entered human hearts. The mission of Islam is the liberation of humankind. "The object of this religion is all humanity and its sphere of action the whole earth." Do these scholars think that if the first three caliphs "had been satisfied that the Roman and the Persian powers were not going to attack the Arabian Peninsula, they would not have striven to spread the message of Islam throughout the world?"[25] Within the frame of Qutb's Islam, this is a knockdown argument. The peace that Islam desires is not the security of the homeland but the "obedience of all people" to "God alone."

Qutb is also aware that during the period when Muhammad was preaching in Mecca, or in the early days of Medina, there is no reference in the Qur'an to violent jihad. In explanation, he argues that in His wisdom God revealed His word in stages. The verses of the sword, as they are called, that begin to appear in the Qur'an during the period of Medina, abrogated the earlier apparently pacific verses. The Qur'an reflects the fact that jihad in the golden age of Islam passed through three stages— in Mecca, the exercise of restraint; in early Medina, warfare, but only against those who fight Islam; finally, war against all "polytheists." This third stage of war against those who reject the sovereignty of God is permanent and "eternal." "Truth and falsehood cannot exist on this earth."[26]

The task awaiting Qutb's tiny Muslim vanguard is vast. He offers his reader a tour of the contemporary world to demonstrate that "all societies existing in the world today are *jahili*."[27] Atheistic communist societies deny people their "spiritual needs," reducing them "to the level of an animal or even a machine." "Idolatrous societies," like India or Japan or what Qutb calls Africa, worship many gods, not God. Jewish and Christian societies, too, deny the Oneness of God, worshipping the Trinity in the case of the Christians and (puzzlingly) Ezra in the case of the Jews, while giving their human assemblies or their rabbis and priests "the authority to make laws." They thus repudiate the sovereignty of God.[28] What, then, of the Islamic societies? Here, Qutb makes his most radical move, his break with all his Islamic contemporaries. "All the existing so-called Muslim societies in the world today are *jahili*." Their way of life is not based upon "submission to God alone." "[T]hey make whatever laws they please and then say: 'This is the Shari'a of God.'" Islam has no option. It must look at all supposedly Muslim societies as "unIslamic and illegal," as sunk in *jahiliyya*.[29]

The revered leader of the Muslim Brotherhood, Hassan al-Banna, never made a claim of this kind about Egypt. The Islamic thinker on whom Qutb drew for the idea of *jahiliyya*, Maududi, regarded contemporary Muslim societies as part-Islamic and part-*jahili*. Eventually this allowed him to participate in Pakistani parliamentary politics. Qutb would have none of this. No society in his view can be "half-Islam and half-*jahiliyya*."[30] This thought pushed Qutb and his followers to the necessity of revolution. It is most likely these sentences that led him, after interrogation, to the gallows.

In urging the vanguard to build an Islamic society where presently none exists, the stakes could not be higher. Either human-kind will be sunk in darkness forever or it will be redeemed. The reasons are many. God gave humankind the sharia. The human law, the sharia, places man in harmony with what Qutb calls "the universal law." Without total submission to the sharia, the creation of the healthy and balanced human person—or, in one more radical formulation, the creation of the only kind of being deserving of the name human—is inconceivable. This is so because total obedience to the sharia is the only way in which "the physical laws which are operative in the biological life of a man and the moral laws which govern his voluntary actions" can be harmonized. In turn, without the emergence under Islam of the fully human person, there can be no good society. When man "makes peace with his own nature, peace and cooperation among individuals follow automatically." When, however, man follows his "desires," "discord" and "conflict" are inevitable. "Desire" is the enemy of the healthy human personality and the spiritual and psychological source of the darkness enveloping the earth. In one striking formulation: "The tree of Islam has been sown and nurtured by the wisdom of God, while the tree of Jahiliyyah is the product of the soil of human desires." And in another: "Command belongs to God, or otherwise to Jahiliyyah; [either] God's Shari'a will prevail, or else people's desires."[31] Here, as in many passages of *Milestones*, the disruptive power of sex lies just beneath the surface.

For Qutb, there is no such thing as a common human culture. The Jews pretend that culture is the heritage of human-kind. This is because they hope to insinuate themselves into all governments and societies so as to take control of the world's financial institutions and to spread the evil practice of usury.

(As with all Salafi jihadists, Qutb is not merely anti-Zionist but deeply anti-Semitic. In the early 1950s Qutb had published "Our Struggle against the Jews," which drew on the analysis of world politics offered by *The Protocols of the Elders of Zion.*[32]) It is true that Muslims can learn from the pure sciences. But they must reject all Western thinking in the fields of the speculative sciences, like Darwinism, or the human sciences, whose conclusions the sharia renders both "ridiculous and absurd." Culture is either Islamic or *jahili.* The ambition of Western culture is to destroy Islam.[33]

Because its values are "permanent and universal," "flexible" but not "fluid," "eternal and unchangeable," Islam alone can civilize any society "whatever the level of industrial and scientific progress."[34] Islam is not indifferent to industrial development or scientific knowledge. However, the societies of the capitalist West and the communist East, despite their material prosperity (in which, Qutb concedes, they are hundreds of years ahead of the present Muslim societies) and their scientific genius (which Qutb claims originated in the empirical methodology of the Islamic universities of Andalusia and the East but has since become "inert" in the supposedly Muslim world) are all "backward."

Civilization in the capitalist West is nothing but "a rubbish heap." Qutb takes what he regards as sexual disorder, which he first observed during his sojourn in the United States, as his primary example. In America people accept the crazed idea they call "the free mixing of the sexes" and behave "like animals." A woman becomes a hostess or a stewardess rather than playing her prescribed role "in the training of human beings." In the Profumo affair, British opinion was shocked not on moral but on Cold War grounds; not because Christine Keeler was a prostitute but because one of her clients was a British cabinet minister and another a Soviet naval attaché. In *jahili* societies "illegitimate sexual relationships, even homosexuality, are not considered immoral."[35] Sexual and family relations "determine the whole character of a society." "Societies which give ascendance to physical desires and animalistic morals cannot be considered civilized." There is, however, a deeper reason why Islam alone can create a civilized society. Because it is founded upon nothing but shared belief, "black and white and red and yellow, Arabs and Greeks and Persians, and all nations which inhabit the earth become one community."[36]

Qutb's imagined Islamic civilization—a prefiguring of the idea of the *umma* found in Salafi jihadism—is not only deterritorialized, to borrow Olivier Roy's formulation, but also deracinated, detribalized, and detached from the blood ties of family.[37] Qutb describes the bonds of race, nation, territory, tribe, and family as "residues of the primitive state of man ... jahili groupings ... from the period when man's spiritual values were at a low stage." He tells us that Muhammad called them "'dead things' against which man's spirit should revolt." With Islam "this partisanship—the partisanship of lineage—ended; and this slogan—the slogan of race—died; and the pride—the pride of nationality—vanished. And man's spirit soared to higher horizons, freed from the bondage of flesh and blood and the pride of soil and country. From that day, the Muslims' home has not been a piece of land, but the homeland of Islam." Qutb encapsulates the imagined Islamic community in a single formula: "Nationalism here is belief; homeland here is *Dar-ul-Islam* [the Abode of Islam]; the ruler here is God; and the constitution here is the Qur'an." In this imagined community of the *umma*, Muslims are "God's representatives on earth." They are freed "from the ties of earth so they might soar toward the skies." They take their place in the universe even "higher than the angels." From there, they look down upon *jahili* individuals wallowing in "mud and dirt."[38] From this place they are not only deterritorialized, deracinated, and detribalized, but somehow also disembodied.

The vanguard must now prepare themselves to struggle in the service of God to create such a world. Qutb speaks to those he hopes will follow him directly. They must recognize that what they are fighting for are not minor changes but revolutionary transformation. "The change from this *jahiliyya*, which has encompassed the earth, to Islam is vast and far-reaching." This is no reason to lose heart. People are only likely to alter their habits if they realize the stakes are of the highest order. The vanguard must speak the truth about the superiority of Islam, as Qutb recalls he did while he was in the United States, clearly and loudly, without defensiveness or deception, ambiguity or embarrassment. Qutb reminds his vanguard of the history of Muhammad at Mecca. The circumstances now appear no more favorable than they did then.

At first, people will flee from the message, as they did at the time of Muhammad. "Then what happened?" "They loved the same truth which at first seemed so strange." The vanguard must never pollute the call by political admixtures coming from the *jahili* world. He warns them against the ideas of Islamic democracy and Islamic socialism. Qutb warns also that they will be advised, presumably by the Egyptian left, to turn their struggle from religion to economic or political or racial struggle. The purpose is to sow confusion. The struggle they are fighting is for the victory of Islam and nothing else.[39]

Qutb explains the motives of the left-wing critics of the Islamic cause with a curious inversion of Marxism. While the left now interpret the medieval Crusades as imperialism in disguise, in reality, he argues, it is rather nineteenth- and twentieth-century imperialists who have tried to disguise with a respectable economic motive the persistence of their deepest desire—the destruction of Islam. In Qutb's view it is not the assertion of economic interest but the struggle of ideas—either true or false, good or evil—that provides the key to the understanding of history.[40] His historical vision is not materialist but idealist, although for him and, indeed, for the entire Salafi jihadist school, the only ideas that ultimately matter in the struggle for mastery of the world are those connected to religion.

Qutb calls his penultimate chapter "The Faith Triumphant."[41] The Believers should never forget that their faith "is bright, clear, beautiful and balanced" and that "the glory of their faith shines forth as never before." Nor should they forget that despite the military and economic humiliation visited upon the Muslim world in recent centuries, those who hold true belief in their hearts have never surrendered their higher human status. "Conditions change, the Muslim loses his physical power and is conquered; yet the consciousness does not depart from him that he is most superior. If he remains a Believer, he looks upon his conqueror from a superior position. He remains certain that this is a temporary condition which will pass away and that faith will turn the tide from which there is no escape."[42] One common orientalist interpretation of recent Islamic history, and indeed of the emergence of Salafi jihadism, focuses on prolonged humiliation of a once proud civilization, and its political and psychological consequences.[43] In this consolatory passage, Qutb provides at least some evidence in its favor.

Qutb begins his final chapter with a vivid Qur'anic story, "The Makers of the Pit," about the ferocious punishment certain Believers experienced. Their faith lifted them above persecution. "They never recanted and burned in the fire until death." Meanwhile, their tormentors—"arrogant, mischievous, criminal and degraded people"—watched even as children, young women, or old men were cast into the fire. Qutb tells this story as a warning to his followers of what they will endure. He warns them that they must not expect that their struggles will succeed in their own lifetimes. God's will is mysterious. Sometimes He punishes wrongdoers; sometimes He does not. Sometimes the meaning of events will be revealed only several generations after they have occurred. Believers can anticipate "contentment of heart"; "the praise of the angels"; as martyrs, "Heaven in the Hereafter"; and, above all else, "the pleasure of God." Only, however, when they understand that rewards are not of this earth will they be able to understand "the milestones" they encounter along the road—"ever paved with skulls and limbs and blood"—that they must travel until death.[44]

Most scholars regard Sayyid Qutb as the twentieth-century father of the political movement now called Salafi jihadism. Gilles Kepel describes him as its "greatest ideological influence"; John Esposito as its "architect."[45] Only Maududi—who was translated into Arabic by Sayyid Abu Hassan Nadwi, one of his disciples and a friend of Qutb—is sometimes thought to be of equal importance, although it has been argued that he for the most part influenced the Arab Salafi jihadists indirectly, rather than directly, through the writings of Qutb.[46] Nor is there doubt about the impact of Qutb's writings on all of the key Salafi jihadist thinkers. In the years following his hanging, a number of underground Islamist revolutionary movements formed in Egypt—Salih Siriyya's Military Technological Academy, Shukri Mustafa's Society of Muslims, Abd al-Salam Faraj's al-Jihad. For all of them, according to Gilles Kepel, John Calvert, and Adnan Musallan, Qutb's work, and in particular *Milestones*, was seminal.[47]

Qutb was also the most influential contemporary author for Abdullah Azzam, the man who inspired and led the Arab mujahidin during the war against the Soviet Army in Afghanistan.[48] In one of his most influential calls to arms, *Join the Caravan*, he quotes a passage from Qutb's *In the Shade of the Qur'an* on the individual duty of all Muslims to undertake jihad. "If Jihad had been a transitory phenomenon in the life of the Muslim Umma, all these sections of the Qur'anic text would not be flooded by this kind of verse! ... If Jihad were a passing phenomenon of Islam, the Messenger of Allah ... would not have said the following words to every Muslim until the Day of Judgment, 'Whoever dies never having fought (in Jihad), nor in having made up his mind to do so, dies on a branch of hypocrisy.'"[49] Osama bin Laden was educated at the King Abdul University in Jeddah, where he attended the lectures of Qutb's loyal brother, Muhammad, the man most responsible for spreading Qutb's influence to a young generation in Saudi Arabia. Bin Laden's closest friend from that time, Mohammed Jamal Khalifa, recalls: "We read Sayyid Qutb.

He was the one who most affected our generation." Qutb's *In the Shade of the Qur'an* and *Milestones* were, according to Lawrence Wright, "the books that would change their lives."[50] The most definitive statement of all, however, regarding the central place of Qutb in the ideological origins of Salafi jihadism can be found in *Knights under the Prophet's Banner*, the late 2001 memoir of Osama bin Laden's deputy, Ayman al-Zawahiri. "Sayyid Qutb's call for loyalty to Allah's Oneness and to acknowledge Allah's sole authority and sovereignty was the spark that ignited the Islamic revolution against the enemies of Islam at home and abroad."[51]

Qutb's seminal role in the origins of the Salafi jihadist movement in the second half of the twentieth century cannot seriously be doubted. There are, however, certain paradoxes in his thought that created uncertainty among his followers.

"What is to be done?" is the most fundamental of all political questions. With Qutb, the answer to that question is rather ambiguous. When writing about jihad in general, as the interpreter of the meaning of the Qur'an, Qutb is an unequivocal advocate of violence in the service of God and the Islamic faith. When, however, he turns his attention to the immediate tasks confronting his followers in Egypt and the contemporary Muslim world, his advice is "patience," spiritual or—as some believed—physical separation, and the building of a community of true Muslims, drinking from the pure waters of the Qur'an so as to allow its great truth to enter their hearts and minds. The present generation of Muslims find themselves in the situation that faced Muhammad and his companions in Mecca. There the challenge, at a time of weakness, was to perfect their own souls and to spread their message through forthright and courageous preaching in the face of torment and persecution.

So it is in contemporary Nasserite Egypt. Eventually, Islam will have to use violence to break down the obstacles inhibiting human beings from exercising their freedom to choose the only true faith. In the immediate future, the task of the Believers is to purify their hearts and to build through *da'wah* (preaching) a community of the faithful. When Qutb advised the Ghazali group to exercise caution and to take up arms only in the defense of their community, he was being neither inconsistent nor hypocritical. The paradox was that he had gathered his following among youthful radicals largely because of his stirring words about spreading the faith through violent jihad, found at length in *In the Shade of the Qur'an* and, more pithily, in *Milestones.*

This points to the second paradox in Qutb. His most radical thought was the claim that all contemporary supposedly Islamic societies had fallen into *jahiliyya,* the terrible darkness humankind experiences in the absence of God. If *jahiliyya* had enveloped the whole society, apart from the vanguard, Qutb appeared to believe that all supposed Muslims lived outside the faith. Within the Islamic tradition this was an extremely dangerous idea. In the early days of Islam, the Kharijite sect emerged, and some of its members accused the rulers of apostasy. Some went further and spread the accusation to the people. They excommunicated not only the rulers but their entire communities. These Kharijites became known as excommunicators, *takfiris.* For the next 1,400 years one of the most serious accusations one Muslim could raise against another was of following in the path of the Kharijites and having become a *takfiri.* This was the charge Qutb faced after his death. In answer, his supporters claimed that he had not excommunicated supposed Muslims as apostates but merely pointed out that, as members of *jahili* societies, through no fault of their own, they were ignorant.[52] This defense, however, left the revolutionary followers of Qutb in an awkward position. Their inclination was toward armed jihad. The logic of Qutb's most radical argument was, however, present political moderation. Therefore, until the society of Muslims was reborn through separation and preaching, the time for spreading the faith by violent jihad had not yet arrived. As we shall see, one tendency among revolutionary followers of Qutb overcame this problem by ignoring his logic and by concentrating instead on the violent removal of the apostate leaders of the *jahili* societies, the so-called *taghuts*, in the belief that this was the road toward the re-creation of a truly Muslim society.

There is another Qutbian paradox, in this instance not discovered within the logic of his argument but the discrepancy between his violent message and his gentle nature. Qutb provided the spark that inspired a generation of radical Muslims to practice violent jihad. Yet there is ample evidence to suggest that he was disturbed when he experienced or even imagined violence. In the United States Qutb described the more physical sports he observed with revulsion. "Football, boxing and wrestling are tantamount to hitting in the belly, breaking arms and legs with all violence and fierceness and the crowds shouting, each encouraging his team: smash his head, break his neck, crush his ribs, knead him into dough."[53] Gilles Kepel tells us that according to several witnesses the barbarity of the prison guards Qutb observed in the slaughter of 1957 provided the psychological foundation for the radicalization of his politics and his hatred of the barbarous regime of President Nasser.[54]

Even when Qutb's intellect was fully engaged with the passages in the Qur'an describing violent jihad, he emphasized the humanity of the Islamic war ethic. In volume 8 of *In the Shade of the Qur'an*, he reminded his readers of one hadith where the Prophet, on discovering that a woman had been killed during one of his expeditions, issued an order forbidding the killing of women and children. In the Islamic ethic of war, he argued, "kind treatment is extended even to enemies ... [Islam] has nothing of the barbarism against children, women or elderly people ... or the disfigurement of dead bodies."[55] Qutb concludes his account of "The Makers of the Pit" with these words: "These criminals sat by the pit of fire, watching how the Believers suffered and writhed in pain. They sat there to enjoy the sight of how fire consumes living beings and how the bodies of these noble souls were reduced to cinder and ashes. And when some young man or woman, some child or old man from among the righteous Believers was thrown into the fire their diabolical pleasure would reach a new height, and shouts of mad joy would escape their lips at the sight of blood and pieces of flesh."[56] When I read this passage I thought of the video the Islamic State distributed which showed to the world a caged Jordanian pilot being burned to death. Between Sayyid Qutb and the Islamic State two changes have to take place within the tradition of Salafi jihadism. A new jurisprudence and ethic of jihad has to be developed and a new hardened and brutalized psychological type has to be born.

None of this is meant to challenge Calvert's description of Qutb as a "dangerous" thinker.[57] Qutb thought only in Manichaean absolutes, with no grey zone of complexity in between—truth or falsity; good or evil; the sovereignty of God or the sovereignty of Man; Islam or *jahiliyya*. He advocated violent jihad and permanent warfare between Islam and the *jahili* societies until the End of Days. Qutb called upon Muslims to give their lives to the ambition of world conquest, which he regarded as the highest moral obligation that was asked of them. He did not understand that the attempt to drive the crooked timber of humanity toward an imagined utopia invariably ends in tragedy. He was also apparently untroubled by doubt. Because he was a wonderful writer, he was able to intoxicate two succeeding generations of Salafi jihadists with his vision. Above all, he did not understand that the hope of re-creating an imagined seventh-century society in the middle of the twentieth century was mad. Qutb was not responsible for the Islamic State. But he posted the first milestone on the road that would eventually lead there.

CHAPTER 3

THE NEGLECTED DUTY— MUHAMMAD ABD AL-SALAM FARAJ

I n the decade and a half following the execution of Sayyid Qutb, his Egyptian followers divided into two broad tendencies, reflecting the ambiguity at the core of his political message. Both groups embraced his idea of the need for a revolutionary vanguard of the faithful if an Islamic state was to be born. One group was most influenced by Qutb's concepts of a world sunk in *jahiliyya* and the requirement, in the present historical Meccan "stage of weakness," for separation. This tendency was represented by a group that called itself the Society of Muslims. Its enemies in the Egyptian state and the Islamic scholarly community, the *ulema*, called it "*Takfir wal Hijra*"— "Excommunication and Withdrawal." The other group was most influenced by Qutb's advocacy of violent jihad, denying that the contemporary situation could be characterized as a stage of weakness and restricting the idea of *jahiliyya* to the *taghut* rulers and their cadre of civil and religious supporters. They believed that an Islamic state would be re-created if the *taghut* leadership was overthrown, either by a coup d'état or a popular uprising or by a popular uprising triggered by a coup d'état. This tendency was represented by the group that called itself—and was called by its enemies—al-Jihad.

The Society of Muslims was the brainchild of an agronomist, Shukri Mustafa, who had been imprisoned at the time of the 1965 state repression and who had spent his period of imprisonment absorbing the writings of Qutb and Maududi before his release in 1971. Shukri built a movement on the basis of the excommunication of society and physical separation from *jahili* society, first in the caves of Asyut province and later in modest, low-rent, so-called "furnished apartments" in Cairo. Shukri's followers believed they were living in an era equivalent to that of Muhammad and his companions in Mecca. They believed their movement of faithful Muslims would become sufficiently strong to conquer and Islamize *jahili* society. The political strategy of the Society of Muslims was summarized by an observer, Saad Eddin Ibrahim: "After its completion, this Islamic community of believers would grow in numbers and in spiritual and material strength. When it had reached a certain point the true believers would march onward bringing down the crumbling social order of Egypt at large."[1]

At first, according to Gilles Kepel, the Shukri group was not taken particularly seriously, except by the parents of the children, especially the daughters, who joined the Society of Muslims. However, in 1976, the Society, as with so many separatist sects, began to fall apart, with one group of defectors trying to lure away members loyal to Shukri. Shukri declared the defectors apostates and conducted a series of assassination raids. The state then finally took them seriously. In response to the crackdown, the Society in July 1977 kidnapped a former Minister of Religion, Muhammad al-Dhahabi, who had described them as Kharijites. It published a series of often extravagant ransom demands, including a Shukri pamphlet, *The Caliphate.*

When the ransom demands were refused, Shukri ordered the murder of al-Dhahabi. Shukri and four of his followers were executed. The Society of Muslims collapsed. Among the followers of Qutb, the idea of excommunication and withdrawal played no further part in history.[2]

The future of the radical Islamist movement in Egypt belonged to the second post-Qutbian tendency, of which the most important expression was the al-Jihad group and the most important early member the electrical engineer Muhammad Abd al-Salam Faraj. At its origins in the late 1970s, al-Jihad was a decentralized, underground revolutionary movement. Its strategy for the Islamization of Egypt was a popular uprising triggered by the removal of the apostate leadership. Its most important deed was the assassination of the Egyptian president, Anwar Sadat, on October 6, 1981.

A fortnight before a military parade celebrating the eighth anniversary of the early victories against Israel in the Yom Kippur War, a member of al-Jihad, Lieutenant Khalid al-Islambouli, learned that his brother had been arrested. Islambouli was due to attend the parade as part of his military duties. He convinced fellow members of al-Jihad to improvise an assassination plan. Faraj helped to procure weapons. Islambouli, who had managed to replace three soldiers in their military vehicle with supporters of al-Jihad, sprayed the presidential party with bullets and proclaimed to the gathering: "I am Khalid al-Islambouli. I have killed the Pharaoh, and I do not fear death." The assassination of Sadat was filmed by an American television crew.

Some members of al-Jihad had anticipated a popular uprising. Cairo, however, remained quiet. A massive regime crackdown followed. In their investigations, the police discovered an unpublished pamphlet written by Faraj, entitled *The Neglected Duty*. According to the Dutch scholar who translated and analyzed the pamphlet, Johannes J. G. Jansen, it was a kind of working paper addressed to fellow members of the Islamist revolutionary underground, most likely written in 1980. On January 3, 1982, the grand mufti of Egypt published a fatwa condemning *The Neglected Duty*. Islambouli, his three military companions, and Faraj were executed in March 1982.[3]

The Neglected Duty was the most important political analysis produced within the revolutionary jihadist movement following Qutb's *Milestones* of 1964. The message of *The Neglected Duty* is buried in quotations from the Qur'an, the hadiths, and the leading medieval Islamic scholars, most importantly Ibn Taymiyya. However, when its central argument is eventually extricated from the thicket, it is remarkably coherent. As this argument helped shape the general course of jihadist politics in Egypt until the late 1990s, it is worth examining in some detail.

According to Faraj, jihad in God's cause is a clear religious duty of Muslims—no less clear than the five pillars of the faith: testifying to the Oneness of God, prayer, payment of the charitable tax, fasting, and pilgrimage to Mecca. As the Prophet put it, jihad is "the best of the summit of Islam."[4] Scandalously, in recent times, jihad has been neglected. This explains the present plight of Islam. "Neglecting jihad is the cause of the lowness, humiliation, division and fragmentation in which the Muslims live today."[5] For this neglect, Faraj primarily blames the *ulema,* the scholars, "who have feigned ignorance of it, but they know that it is the only way to the return and the establishment of the glory of Islam anew."[6] Nor is Faraj in any doubt as to the nature of jihad. Like Qutb, he regards jihad as violent struggle in God's cause, or what he calls "struggle by the sword."[7] To prove this point, Faraj considers alternative readings of jihad. One suggestion is that jihad passes through three "successive stages": first, the struggle to perfect one's own soul; then, the struggle against the devil; finally, the struggle against infidels and hypocrites. Faraj dismisses this argument with contempt. These are aspects, not stages, of jihad. If they were stages, one would have to postpone the struggle against the devil! Only people of "complete ignorance or excessive cowardice" argue like this.[8] What then of the hadith that attributes to Muhammad the view that the struggle against one's soul is the greater jihad and the struggle against infidels and apostates the lesser form? According to Faraj, it is widely known that this hadith is a "fabrication."[9] The purpose of the fabrication is to wrest the sword from the hand of the Muslim. Faraj invests violent jihad with considerable pathos. He quotes a poet-scholar: "Some people make their cheeks wet with tears / in great quantities / but our chests and throats become wet by torrents of our blood."[10]

What, then, is the purpose of violent jihad? It is to free Islam from its present humiliation by re-creating the caliphate destroyed in 1924. The portents are promising. Faraj points to a hadith that prophesies first the prophethood, then a caliphate, then a kingship that "hinders," then a kingship that "compels," and finally the return of the caliphate, "equal (in righteousness) to the Prophethood." Egypt is at present under a kingship that compels—the presidential regimes of Nasser and Sadat, who rose to power by a "military coup."[11] The restoration of the caliphate now awaits.

To re-create the caliphate, however, a true Islamic state, or what Faraj calls a "territorial nucleus," has first to exist.[12] Like Qutb, Faraj is convinced that in the present era there is no Islamic state—that is to say, a state ruled by Islamic law.[13] Faraj turns to Ibn Taymiyya's description of Mongol rule over Muslims. The Mongols combined their own law with parts of the sharia, with Jewish and Christian law, and with ideas that took the fancy of Genghis Khan.[14] Contemporary Egypt is in an almost identical situation. It is ruled by laws imposed on it by infidels. The present Egyptian leaders fast and pray, pretending to be Muslims. However, having been "raised at the tables of Imperialism, be it Crusaderism, Communism, or Zionism," they have nothing in common with Islam except the name. As the study of Ibn Taymiyya makes clear, the Egyptian leaders are worse than infidels. Having been inside the faith and having abandoned it, they are "apostates."[15] Nor is it only the leaders who are condemned. So are their principal servants. One of the Mongols' viziers, Rashid al-Din, implied that Muhammad did not want Jews and Christians to give up their religion. The current servants of the Egyptian leadership speak of "Religious Brotherhood" or, even worse, of the "Unity of Religions."[16] Unlike Qutb or Shukri, however—and this is fundamentally important to his revolutionary plan of action—Faraj believes that the people of Egypt can straightforwardly be described as Muslims. There is no need for delay while Islam is restored to society. "The State (of Egypt) in which we live today is ruled by the Laws of Disbelief although the majority of its inhabitants are Muslims."[17] The conclusion is clear. If a caliphate is to be re-created, if an Islamic state is to come into being from which the caliphate can emerge, it is the duty of Muslims to remove the leadership of Egypt through violent jihad.

To strengthen his case, Faraj considers possible objections. The first comes from Qutb implicitly, and in Faraj's own day explicitly from Shukri, both of whom thought Muslims were in the situation that once confronted Muhammad and his companions in Mecca. As such, before an Islamic state could be born through jihad, true Muslims had to separate themselves from the surrounding *jahili* society and form a movement that would eventually bring society to Islam. Faraj dismisses this Meccan escape clause. He points out that while still in Mecca, Muhammad warned the Quraysh tribe: "I bring you slaughter."[18] If Muslims were now in the Meccan stage, they would have to foreswear prayers and fasting or agree to usury, all emerging from later post-Meccan Qur'anic revelations.[19] Although he does not mention them by name, he is openly contemptuous of Shukri, who was hanged two years earlier, and his Society of Muslims. "There are . . . those who say that they will emigrate to the deserts and then come back and have a confrontation with the Pharaoh." This is simply a way of avoiding the only "true road—fighting."[20] In the supposed Meccan stage of weakness, is it not foolhardy to engage in combat? According to Faraj, this argument makes no sense. "How can this strength be realized when you abolish the duty of jihad?"[21]

Is violent jihad the only means by which an Islamic state in Egypt can be created? Faraj conducts a scathing *tour d'horizon* of all contemporary alternative approaches. Muslim benevolent societies leave the status quo intact. They even have to register with the apostate state. Indirectly, in reference to the strategic drift of the Muslim Brotherhood, he concedes that building an Islamic political party might be preferable to creating a benevolent society, but it involves both collaboration with "the pagan state" and acceptance of law-making assemblies that deny the sovereignty of God. Some say that "politics hardens the heart and keeps people away from remembering God." People who say this do not understand Islam and are in reality cowards. The existing system will not somehow "perish automatically" by filling elite positions with Muslims. Indeed, the pagan state will never permit a Muslim to be appointed to a truly influential position.

Nor will preaching, *da'wah*, by itself ever be enough. Only a "believing minority" can create the Islamic state. Majority support is not needed. Moreover, preaching will not disturb the propaganda made possible by the state's control over the means of mass communication. Not only will religious piety and obedience by themselves change nothing, Islam makes clear that the highest form of devotion is jihad. No doubt the pursuit of knowledge is admirable, but it is both a lesser obligation than jihad and impotent in the face of power. Faraj reminds his fellow revolutionaries of the time when "Napoleon and his soldiers entered al-Azhar [University] on horseback. What did their knowledge help against that comedy?"[22]

What kind of obligation is violent jihad? Traditional Islamic jurisprudence distinguishes between those obligations that are collective and ordered by authority, *fard kifaya*, which can be fulfilled by a community, and those that are individual, *fard ayn*, like praying and fasting. According to Faraj, there are three circumstances where participation in jihad is *fard ayn*, an individual obligation—during battle a soldier cannot desert; if an Islamic territory is under attack, it must be defended;

if a leader gives an order, it must be obeyed. As jihad is an individual obligation, according to Islamic jurisprudence it releases children from the obligation to obey their parents.[23] For an Islamist underground movement whose members are asked to risk their lives, a theological argument that liberates young Muslims of faith from the control of their parents is a revolutionary asset of some significance.

At this point, Faraj makes several rather swashbuckling argumentative moves fundamental to the future of Salafi jihadism, clearing the decks of centuries of inconvenient Islamic legal thinking apparently inhibiting armed or revolutionary jihad.

Do Muslims have the right to rebel against their rulers? Faraj answers this grave question in a single sentence. "When (a Leader) suddenly becomes an unbeliever, his leadership comes to an end."[24] Is armed jihad legitimate without an order from a caliph or a commander? According to Faraj, Islam makes clear that from even a party of three a leader, an *amir*, selected on the basis of merit can emerge.[25] How should Muslims forced to fight in an army of infidels conduct themselves? Faraj suggests that it is their duty to abandon arms and allow themselves to be killed. Can Muslims, alternatively, take the lives of fellow Muslims in the course of battle? Faraj has no doubt they can. Muslims who die while fighting on the side of infidels or apostates will be rewarded in the Hereafter.[26] What fate awaits the Muslims who engage in battle? If they survive, they will return home with the booty permitted by the sharia. If they die, they will receive the rewards a hadith—which would from now on enter the canon of Salafi jihadist thought—promised to martyrs: "He will be forgiven upon the first drop of blood. His seat will be in Paradise. He will be free from the punishment of the grave. He will be safe from the Great Fright. He will marry the heavenly dark-eyed virgins. He will intercede for 70 of his relatives."[27]

Can jihadists engage in deception? Faraj argues that they can.[28] Can they lie? According to Faraj, the answer is yes, although it is preferable, if possible, to speak with ambiguity.[29] Can jihadists ally with infidels? Faraj argues that they can, but only so long as the infidel has a "good opinion" of Muslims.[30] Can Islam be spread by the sword? Faraj does not object to the phrase that Qutb regarded as "a vicious slander," although he agrees with Qutb that the purpose of raising "the sword" is not to force belief but to slay rulers who "hide the Truth," preventing it from entering "the hearts of Men."[31] Can infidels be killed for their words? Faraj cites the case of a Jewish leader, free of crime or misdeed, of whom the Prophet said: "He mocked Us with poetry, and not one of you has ever done this without having the sword as punishment."[32] (One thinks of filmmaker Theo van Gogh or the satirists at *Charlie Hebdo*.) Can women and children be killed in battle? Faraj is aware of the hadith cited by Qutb, but he brings an alternative to the table, in which Muhammad justified taking the lives of women and children on the ground that "they are part of their fathers."[33] (One thinks of 9/11, the Shi'a neighborhoods of Baghdad, and the promenade at Nice.)

Faraj is not exclusively concerned with such general problems of law and theory. He discusses two pressing practical and controversial political questions being discussed at the time in al-Jihad circles.

If the president of Egypt is assassinated, will that lead to the creation of an Islamic state? Faraj's answer is worth quoting in detail. "It is said that we fear establishing the State (because) after one or two days a reaction will occur that will put an end to everything we have accomplished. The refutation of this [view] is that the establishment of an Islamic State is the execution of a divine Command. We are not responsible for its results. Someone who is so stupid as to hold this view ... forgets that when the Rule of the Infidel has fallen everything will be in the hands of the Muslims, whereupon the downfall of the Islamic State will be inconceivable."[34] As Faraj soon learned, the stupid skeptics were entirely right. The reaction did occur. The consequence of the assassination of Sadat was not a popular uprising and the birth of the Islamic state in Egypt, but mass state repression and his own execution.[35] Faraj's belief that the revolutionaries were not responsible for the aftermath of the assassination and that their victory was assured because it aligned with God's command is eloquent testimony to how primitive and naive the political thinking of the jihadist revolutionaries was at this stage in their history.

Faraj also provided a clear answer to a political question of equal significance that divided the members of the Egyptian revolutionary Islamist underground. Should the movement concentrate on the struggle against their own apostate leaders—who Faraj called "the near enemy"—or should they give priority to the struggle to destroy the Jewish state of Israel—"the far enemy"? "It is true," Faraj argued, "that the liberation of the Holy Land is a religious command, obligatory on all Muslims." But it was also true that Muhammad regarded prudence and an understanding of priorities, of "what is useful and harmful," as a characteristic of the believer. Faraj provided two main reasons for fighting the near enemy first. In the case of a struggle against either the near or the far enemy, Muslim blood would be spilled, but only in the case of victory over the near enemy would an Islamic state be created. The stranglehold of imperialism in the Muslim lands, moreover, relied on their apostate client regimes. Fighting the far enemy first, while their apostate clients continued to exist, would prove "a waste of time."[36] As it happened, Faraj won the near enemy–far enemy argument. For close to two decades the jihadists in Egypt concentrated on their struggle with the state, a strategic argument captured by the slogan "the road to Jerusalem runs through Cairo," which was coined in 1995 by their most important member, Ayman al-Zawahiri. It was only when Zawahiri merged his section of al-Jihad with Osama bin Laden's al-Qaeda in mid-2001 that the priority of the most radical tendency among the Egyptian jihadists became the far enemy—the United States and Israel.

Faraj ended *The Neglected Duty* with a romantic and puritanical character portrait of the knightly jihadist warrior, of a man who would scrutinize his soul with the greatest care to ensure there was not the slightest taint of ego. Faraj tells the story of the man who, fearing for "the sincerity of his devotion to God," veiled his face when going into battle so as to ensure that he was not later praised. The jihadists who fought in order to appear to the world as "courageous," "learned," or "generous" were all condemned to "the fire." Faraj quotes Qutb. The jihadist is the man for whom fighting is "more pleasant and more beautiful" than "spiritless comfort." Even the pious but vain man of religion is not suited to jihad. He should be advised to return to his home for the reason Caliph Umar II once offered: "It is more just if we do not tempt him, he is the pride of the masses." This final story of *The Neglected Duty* provides its only remotely light-hearted moment.[37]

If Sayyid Qutb provided the vision for the tradition of political thought that came to be called Salafi jihadism, Muhammad Abd al-Salam Faraj provided it with its first operational manual. Although like all analogies this one is imperfect, within the ideologies that led, respectively, to the Soviet Union and the Islamic State, Qutb's *Milestones* resembles Marx and Engels's *The Communist Manifesto*, and Faraj's *The Neglected Duty*, Lenin's *What Is to Be Done?* Just as Lenin found arguments which allowed him to sidestep Marx's belief that socialist revolutions leading eventually to communism were made possible by the contradictions of advanced capitalist economies, Faraj rejected Qutb's conviction that before an Islamic state could be created the societies of the supposedly Islamic regimes would have to be brought to the faith by a movement of true Muslims.

Following Faraj's execution, al-Jihad and its ally, al-Gama'a al-Islamiyya, split into two main jihadist movements. Originally the split was over leadership. Eventually it concerned revolutionary strategy, the relationship between popular revolution and military coup d'état. Between 1990 and 1997 both groups waged violent struggle against the regime of Hosni Mubarak, Sadat's successor. Both accepted Faraj's view that the way to create an Islamic state was violent jihad against the near enemy. Eventually the long, complex, and bloody struggle against the Egyptian regime proved fruitless. In July 1997, a group of imprisoned members of al-Gama'a al-Islamiyya agreed to abandon violence. In November, following near-universal popular revulsion with a terrorist massacre at Luxor which killed fifty-eight foreign tourists and four Egyptian citizens, the majority of al-Gama'a al-Islamiyya effectively finally abandoned violent revolution.[38] In 1998 the most significant element of the al-Jihad group, led by Zawahiri, and the remaining jihadi elements of al-Gama'a al-Islamiyya signed an al-Qaeda fatwa which targeted the far enemy—Americans and Jews. Only now was Faraj's legacy exhausted.[39]

Regarding the intellectual origins of the Islamic State, however, a close reading of *The Neglected Duty* provides the first glimpses of arguments that were taken to the center of Salafi jihadism by Abu Musab al-Zarqawi. There was not the slightest hint of sectarian hatred in the writing of Qutb. Indeed, Qutb was translated into Persian and became something of a hero of the Iranian Islamist revolution of 1979, with a stamp bearing his portrait even issued by the Ayatollah Khomeini regime.[40] By contrast there are clear anti-Shi'a references in Faraj. Among the groups that Faraj insisted must be fought were those who disbelieved anything the companions agreed upon during the period of "the rightly guided Caliphs" or who attacked "the great personalities from the earliest generations of Muslims."[41] The Sunni–Shi'a divide begins precisely with the rejection of the first three caliphs. Faraj also supports the bitter hostility found in Ibn Taymiyya. He quotes with approval Taymiyya's description of the *Rafida*, the rejecters, as "belonging to the most evil class of men."[42] There is, too, no trace of apocalyptical or eschatological thinking in Qutb's *Milestones*. In *The Neglected Duty*, Faraj quotes a hadith that inquired whether the victory of Islam would occur first in Constantinople or in Rome. He reminds his readers that 800 years later Constantinople fell to Islam. He assures them that before too long it will also conquer Rome.[43] At another point Faraj refers to the Mahdi, the Islamic Messiah, whose arrival, according to the Islamic apocalyptic tradition, will signal the coming of the Day of Judgment.

As James Toth argues, Qutb did not believe Islam needed "to engage in miracles and 'tricks' that he said Christianity had resorted to in order to attract followers." In *Milestones*, he described God's will as mysterious and unknowable.[44] There is, however, in Faraj one reference to the miracles God will visit upon the earth to assist those waging jihad for the faith. When Muslims and only Muslims are fighting, he argues, "God will intervene and change the laws of nature." In the next stage of the evolution of the tradition of thought that reaches its final destination in the mind of the Islamic State—Abdullah Azzam's global summons to jihad in Afghanistan—the miracles by which God graces his mujahidin assume a surprisingly central role.

CHAPTER 4

JOIN THE CARAVAN— ABDULLAH AZZAM

In 1981, the year President Anwar Sadat was assassinated, Abdullah Azzam, the man who is often described as the father of global jihad, was convinced by a member of the Egyptian Muslim Brotherhood of the significance of the emerging Islamic resistance to the 1979 Soviet invasion of Afghanistan. Azzam left his position at the King Abdulaziz University in Jeddah, Saudi Arabia, for one at Pakistan's International Islamic University in Islamabad. Shortly after, he traveled to Afghanistan, where for the next eight years, until his assassination in November 1989, he fought, preached, wrote, published, organized, raised money, and traveled across the world for the anti-Soviet cause. Without Azzam's call to jihad, it is difficult to imagine that the tens of thousands of Islamic foreign fighters, most significantly Arabs, would have flocked to Afghanistan in the second half of the 1980s. Without these foreign fighters—which included Osama bin Laden, Ayman al-Zawahiri, and Abu Musab al-Zarqawi—it is even more difficult to imagine that Salafi jihadism, the ideology that shapes the mind of the Islamic State, would have assumed the role in history that it has.

Abdullah Azzam was a Palestinian, born in 1941, who grew up in a conservative and reasonably prosperous family in a village on the West Bank of the Jordan River. Azzam was an unusually pious and scholarly child, who was accepted into the Muslim Brotherhood before reaching the required age. In 1966 he graduated from the sharia faculty of the University of Damascus. Following the Israeli occupation of the West Bank in 1967, Azzam moved to the Jordan River's East Bank. To the dismay of his parents, who regarded engagement in jihad as beneath his social status, in 1969 Azzam joined the *fedayeen* as a Palestinian guerrilla fighter. According to a cousin, Azzam exploded at his parents' complaints: "I am inviting you to heaven, and you are inviting me to hell!" Fifteen years later, he would raise the question of the parental right to forbid engagement in jihad in *The Defence of the Muslim Lands*, his fatwa on jihad in Afghanistan. Despite parental disapproval, Azzam joined an Islamic military unit. One of its actions was called "Operation Sayyid Qutb."

Azzam was repelled by the secularism of the Palestine Liberation Front and the impiety of its soldiers. On one occasion he asked a fellow *fedayeen* what the religion behind the Palestinian revolution was, and received a blunt reply. "The revolution has no religion behind it." For Azzam, this was "the final straw." Following the Jordanian monarchy's 1970 anti-*fedayeen* repression, known as Black September, Azzam turned from guerrilla warfare to the life of the scholar.

Between 1970 and 1973 Azzam undertook doctoral studies in Islamic jurisprudence at Egypt's Al-Azhar University. In Cairo, he was close to members of Sayyid Qutb's family and part of a Qutbist political circle. Having completed his doctorate, Azzam was appointed to a post at the University of Jordan. On occasion, he lectured in combat fatigues. In 1979 Azzam was dismissed because of the radicalism of his views.

After brief teaching posts in Jeddah and Islamabad, in 1981 he entered Afghanistan—as an accomplished Islamic scholar and a former *fedayeen*. Azzam fought with the mujahidin—according to his Arab hagiographers, traveling the land on a donkey. He established the mujahidin training camps Sada and Khaldun. He published a monthly magazine, *Al-Jihad*, that was distributed across the *umma* and which called upon the Muslims of the world to participate in jihad in Afghanistan. To raise money, recruits, and awareness of the cause, Azzam traveled extensively, visiting fifty cities in the United States. In the pre-Internet age, videotapes of his fiery and eloquent speeches circulated widely.[1]

In 1984, in collaboration with Osama bin Laden, a wealthy Saudi student of Yemeni origin who had studied briefly with him, Azzam established in Peshawar a logistical guesthouse, the Maktab al-Khidamat, or the Afghan Services Bureau, where Arab jihadist volunteers were housed and trained. In 1986 Azzam and bin Laden parted company. They disagreed about administrative matters and military tactics. Most importantly, however, bin Laden wanted to create separate Arab military units, while Azzam insisted that the Arabs fight alongside Afghans. Bin Laden's al-Qaeda was created as a consequence of their separation. Relations between the two most significant Arab Afghans, as the Arab volunteers were called, nonetheless remained respectful and amicable. In 1986 Azzam supported bin Laden's heroic military debut at the Battle of Jaji, where a Soviet paramilitary force was repelled. He also supported bin Laden's disastrous military action at Jalalabad in mid-1989, where on two days a thousand Arab volunteers or more were slaughtered.[2]

On November 24, 1989, Azzam was assassinated by a roadside bomb on the way to his regular Friday prayers. He quickly joined the vast roll call of martyrs of the Afghan war, whose deaths he had by then done so much to imprint on the imagination of the *umma*. His admirers around the world were told that while the body parts of other passengers, including his two sons, were strewn for a hundred meters, Azzam's body remained intact and exuded a fragrant smell of musk.[3] No one knows who was responsible for the assassination. However, in 1988 and 1989 Azzam had been an active supporter of the new Palestinian Islamist movement, Hamas, advising on its charter and raising funds for it in the United States.[4] One of his collaborators in Afghanistan, the Egyptian jihadist Mustafa Hamid, is convinced that Israeli intelligence agency Mossad was responsible.[5] Azzam once wrote that it was only in the years when he fought in Palestine and Afghanistan that he had been truly alive.

Shortly after his arrival in Afghanistan, Abdullah Azzam wrote his surpassingly strange and romantic *Signs of Ar-Rahmaan [Miracles] in the Jihad of Afghanistan*. For the most part it consists of scores of stories told to Azzam of the miracles that God bestowed on the Afghans in their war against the Soviet Army.[6]

Azzam was told about the very many victories the mujahidin had won despite being hopelessly outnumbered. In one story, fifty-nine mujahidin defeated a communist force of 1,500; in another, 120 routed 10,000 Soviet troops with 800 tanks and twenty-five planes; in yet another, a single rocket destroyed eighty-five tanks and a personnel carrier. He was also told dozens of stories of miraculous escapes. One mujahidin officer was seen "coming off the battlefield with his clothes riddled with bullet holes." He was "untouched." A mine exploded under the foot of a mujahidin; he suffered no injury. In one camp, 300 napalm bombs were dropped and "not a single one exploded."

Azzam heard many stories in which the laws of nature were suspended as a sign of God's grace. In one, the body of an Afghan martyr lit up the sky for exactly three minutes each evening. In several, flocks of birds flew beneath Soviet aircraft—in one case at two or three times the speed of sound—to warn villagers of impending aerial bombardment. Scorpions attacked Soviet troops. "Six of them died and the remainder fled." Several stories concerned wild dogs who devoured the corpses of communist soldiers but never those of Afghans. The bodies of many Afghans who had fallen in battle, like the body of Azzam, were said to have emitted the fragrance of musk or ambergris. Azzam was told on several occasions that long after death, the blood of Afghan martyrs still flowed. Seven months after the imam of an Afghan town was killed by the communists, his body was preserved intact, "except the nose." The grave of a martyr was opened two and a half years after he had been buried. "We found him as he had been, except his beard had grown longer." One mother placed her finger on the wound of her son. Many months later, "her finger emitted the aroma of perfume." Another mother was martyred with her baby. "Some people tried to remove the baby but were unable to separate her from her mother."[7]

According to Azzam, even though these stories resemble

"fairy tales," he heard so many of them from so many "trust-worthy and reliable" sources, that they easily passed the *tawatur*, the rigorous test used to authenticate hadiths, leaving no possibility of "fabrication."[8] In a recent book, *Understanding Apocalyptic Terrorism*, Frances Flannery suggests that these stories indicate that Azzam was a precursor of the kind of eschatological thinking found at the center of the ideology of the Islamic State.[9] This appears to me a category mistake. While apocalyptic thought invariably involves miracles, accounts of miracles frequently do not involve apocalyptic thinking. Azzam's tales of miracles are an expression not of apocalyptic thinking, but of his certainty that God had blessed the Afghans.

Miracles of Jihad is a romance of the Afghan peoples. They are a "primitive, simple nation unspoiled by the winds of modernization." They are also almost unique in their religious fervor. Having asked scores of Afghans lying wounded in hospital, ranging from boys of eleven to men of 102, why they were fighting, all replied that it was to build an Islamic state. Azzam tells of encountering entire regiments of Afghan troops, every one of whom fulfilled their obligation of daily prayers. Not only were the Afghans unusually pious, they were also a nation of fighters—"insubordinate, warrior-like by nature, scorning disgrace and not able to bear injustices." Neither Alexander the Great nor the British Empire was able to subdue the Afghans. Azzam tells the story of 1842, where only one British soldier in Afghanistan survived, from an army of 12,000. "The inability to conquer Afghanistan was in spite of Britain ruling India and Pakistan for two centuries." In his own time, he tells of a leader of the mujahidin who captured five Russian generals and put them to death, refusing to negotiate despite the direst threats of retribution. "We are not merchants." "Where else," Azzam asks in *Miracles*, "will you find a million young men ready for death, whose hearts are kindled with a passion for jihad? Where else will you find a complete army of volunteers, not taking a single rupee?" "Only in Afghanistan."

Before arriving in Afghanistan, Azzam tells his readers, he had merely read about the "abstentious" life of the companions of the Prophet. In Afghanistan, he saw such abstemiousness with his own eyes. He visited the home of one of the leading mujahidin generals, Shaykh Sayyaf. It was made of mud, with sand floors. When the first edition of *Miracles* was published in 1982, only a handful of foreign fighters had joined the Afghan jihad. At this time when the *umma* was still asleep, Azzam met an Afghan soldier who sold his goats and sheep to buy one round of ammunition. He saw mujahidin forced to share shoes whose toes had fallen off because of the snow and ice. Above all, Azzam's romance of the Afghan warrior concerns their character.[10] He wrote later in the decade, "When they love a person, they will give their life and soul for him, and if they dislike him they will not show it at all."[11] Even the landscape somehow mirrored "the strength and pride" of the Afghan mujahidin. "It seems as if the Glorified and Exalted prepared the mountains and the land there especially for jihad."[12]

In the second half of the 1980s, significant numbers of Arabs did indeed respond to Azzam's call to wage jihad in Afghanistan.[13] Some were Salafis from the Wahabbite tradition of Saudi Arabia. Major tensions developed between these Saudi Salafis and Afghans, sometimes, according to Mustafa Hamid, threatening to break into armed conflict.[14] Perhaps in response, Azzam's early idolization of the Afghans was somewhat tempered. In later writing, Azzam considers what he calls the "serious" concerns, most likely of the Saudi Salafis, about the level of education, customs, and religious practices of the Afghans. It is true, he argues, that many Afghans are caught in "the cage of communal practice" and "the accumulation of custom," and that very many are "illiterate." In entire regiments there will be no one able to recite the Qur'an or perform the funeral prayer.[15] Not only do most Afghans follow the Hanafi school of law, very many do not even consider non-Hanafis to be Muslims. Those joining the jihad will encounter disturbing un-Islamic practices like smoking or visiting tombs or wearing talismans.[16]

Azzam answers these Salafi concerns in different ways. The lack of Islamic education only strengthens the need for undertaking the journey to Afghanistan, to help fulfill the religious obligations and educate the Afghans. Those coming to Afghanistan to wage jihad should not only exercise self-restraint but also show "respect [for] the Hanafi school." While there are no doubt many sinful Afghans, is there any Islamic nation on earth, he asks, populated entirely by angels? No Muslim should regard the faults in the religious practices or the customary behavior of the Afghans as grounds for failing to answer the call of jihad.[17] "We must choose from two evils: that Russia takes Afghanistan and turns it into a kaffir [infidel] country and forbids Qur'an and Islam for it. Or, jihad with a nation with sins and errors."[18] And perhaps most importantly of all, whatever their shortcomings, he reminds the Salafis that the Afghans almost alone "have refused disgrace in their religion, and have purchased their dignity with seas of blood and mountains of corpses and lost limbs. Other nations have submitted to colonization and disbelief on the first day." Among all of those who contributed to the evolution of the Salafi jihadist ideology, only Azzam shows what Nelly Lahoud calls "anthropological sensitivity" to religious and cultural differences within the presently existing Muslim world.[19]

In the second half of the 1980s, Abdullah Azzam wrote two influential books about the mujahidin's war against the Soviet Army. The first was his fatwa, *The Defence of the Muslim Lands*, a work that he circulated widely before publication and that won the approval of some scholars in the Islamic world, including the Saudi Arabian Sheikh Abd al-Aziz ibn Baz. The second was his rallying cry to the *umma*, *Join the Caravan*. The fatwa has a formal argumentative structure; *Join the Caravan* a rhetorical power almost unsurpassed in the Salafi jihadist canon. However, as there is considerable overlap in both tone and content, it is best to consider them together.[20]

In *The Defence of the Muslim Lands* and *Join the Caravan* Azzam combines Qutb's pessimism about the sorry state of the *umma* at a time of *jahiliyya* with Faraj's argument about jihad as Islam's neglected duty. For centuries, Azzam argues, jihad, one of the paramount obligations of Islam, has been "forgotten." "Anybody who looks into the state of the Muslims today will find that their greatest misfortune is their abandonment of Jihad. ... Because of that the tyrants have gained dominance over the Muslims in every aspect and every land." Their infidel enemies "only stand in awe of fighting."[21] Jihad is the key, therefore, to the revival of Islam.

In Islamic law, jihad takes two forms. Offensive jihad, which must be fought "until there remains only Muslims or people who submit to Islam," concerns those battles where "the kuffar are not gathering to fight the Muslims." Defensive jihad concerns those battles where the *kuffar* have occupied Muslim lands. Both offensive and defensive jihad are obligatory but they involve obligations of a different kind. Here Azzam follows Faraj and, before him, Hassan al-Banna in his famous essay on jihad.[22] As we have seen, in Islamic law there are two basic forms of obligation. One form can be fulfilled by the community—*fard kifaya*. Others, such as prayer or fasting, are individual obligations—*fard ayn*. Offensive jihad, according to Azzam, is *fard kifaya*; defensive jihad is *fard ayn*.

Azzam's argument about individual obligation involves the idea of the expanding circle. When the infidel enters Muslim lands, the obligation for its defense at first falls upon the population under invasion. If, however, they are unable to offer a successful defense, the obligation falls upon Muslims in neighboring lands. And if their force is insufficient, then it falls upon those more distant. And so on. While the invaders continue to occupy Muslim lands, the obligation "becomes *fard ayn* upon the whole world."[23] The implication of this argument is radical. In the case of an unrepelled enemy invasion of Islamic land, every Muslim in the world acquires an individual obligation, no less solemn than the obligation of prayer or fasting, to engage in jihad to free the land under continuing infidel occupation. Azzam believes contemporary Muslims have been corrupted by their enemies into thinking in terms of the nation-state boundaries the colonizers have imposed upon them. He thinks exclusively in terms of the *umma*. His authority here, as so often in the Salafi jihadist tradition, is Ibn Taymiyya, the scholar he once claimed formed the foundation of his jurisprudential thinking, who argued: "The Muslim lands are like one land."[24]

If an obligation is collective, according to the scholars, before the call can be answered slaves must request permission from their masters, debtors from their creditors, children from their parents.[25] If, however, the obligation is individual, as it is in the case of defensive jihad, no permission is required. Azzam uses the case of a crowd seeing a child drowning. Who would suggest that permission be sought before leaping into the water? "This is the situation of Afghanistan today. She is crying for help, her children are being slaughtered, her women are raped ... and when sincere young men want to save and assist them they are criticized and blamed."[26]

Are there any exceptions to *fard ayn* in the case of defensive jihad? In theory, the obligation does not fall upon children or the aged.[27] In practice, under contemporary conditions with regard to Afghanistan, it also does not fall on those who cannot obtain a passport or who are refused flight on an aircraft. Nor does it fall upon those whose parents or children have no alternative means of support. It does, however, fall on women, so long as they are accompanied by a *mahram*, a man with whom there is no possibility of sexual relations. Once again, Azzam is sensitive to local conditions. Because the women of Afghanistan do not fight, nor should non-Afghans. In Afghanistan there is, however, much work to be done in the fields of education, nursing, and assistance to refugees. Even legitimate fears of police interrogation or intelligence surveillance on return from the battle does not relieve men from their obligations. They can always settle in the land of jihad.[28]

Azzam considers several standard objections to involvement in armed struggle as an individual obligation in the case of the defense of Muslim lands. Some have argued that Muslims are relieved of the obligation in the absence of a caliph, a legitimate leader of the *umma*, with the authority to issue orders. Azzam laughs this argument to scorn. Is it not obvious that it is only through jihad that the caliphate can be restored?[29] Leaders can be selected from the smallest groups of Muslims. Even single individuals are required to fight. Can Muslims fight even when fellow Muslims are used as human shields? Azzam cites authorities to prove that they can.[30] If there is a danger of starvation, should resources for jihad still be accorded priority? On the basis of the same authorities, Azzam argues that they should.[31] Is the purification of the individual soul, however, a higher form of jihad than armed struggle? As with all of the Salafi jihadists, Azzam dismisses as a fabrication the hadith that suggests it is.

Under contemporary conditions, where should defensive jihad concentrate? In Azzam's view, there are two pressing cases: Palestine and Afghanistan. Azzam regards Palestine as ultimately the more important. It is at the very heart of the historical *umma*. Where jihad for the liberation of Palestine from the Jews is possible, it should be waged. On pragmatic grounds, however, he argues that Afghanistan provides the more promising immediate prospect. The battle there is raging. The leaders of the resistance, unlike those of the secular Palestine Liberation Organization, are faithful Muslims. Only in Afghanistan is there an immediate prospect of the creation of an Islamic state. The Palestinian resistance relies on the support of the Soviet Union, a *kuffar* nation. The Afghan mujahidin are independent. In Palestine, there is almost impenetrable security where "the eyes of the authorities spy from all sides for anyone who attempts to infiltrate its borders to kill the Jews." In Afghanistan, there are ideal conditions for jihad: 3,000 kilometers of open borders and many independent tribes.[32]

Can those waging jihad in Afghanistan call upon the assistance of the infidel nations, like the United States? In this instance, as Azzam regards traditional authority as ambiguous, he offers his own opinion. So long as help is truly needed, the Muslims have the upper hand, and the infidels show respect, assistance is acceptable.[33] Can the mujahidin sign a peace treaty with the infidel enemy? Once more Azzam thinks authority is ambiguous. In his opinion, however, a treaty is possible so long as "not a handspan" of Muslim land is relinquished nor unacceptable conditions imposed, such as permitting Jews and Christians to live in the lands of the two holy mosques of Mecca and Medina, or allowing churches to be built or missionaries to preach on Muslim lands.[34] What kind of treaty then might be negotiated with the Russians? All of their troops must be withdrawn. There must be no political conditions. The Russians must recognize the mujahidin as their negotiating partners. They must accept the creation of a truly Islamic state. Looking into the future, Azzam issues a warning. If an Islamic state is indeed created in Afghanistan, it will not be long before hostile Western intervention.[35]

Will the agenda of defense of Muslim lands be exhausted if Afghanistan is cleansed of Russians and Palestine of Jews? It most certainly will not. Azzam provides a list of the once Muslim lands now occupied by the infidels—"the Philippines, Kashmir, Lebanon, Chad, Eritrea, etc."[36] All must eventually be restored to Islam. This is perhaps the most radical idea in *The Defence of the Muslim Lands.* According to Azzam, it is *fard ayn,* individually obligatory for all Muslims, to wage jihad until all formerly Muslim lands are liberated from the infidel occupiers. This is a formula for permanent warfare between Islam and disbelievers into an indefinite future. As offensive war until Islam is victorious everywhere on earth is also obligatory but *fard kifaya,* Azzam also supports a clash of civilizations likely to last for centuries.

Azzam berates his contemporaries. Given that jihad is "the zenith of the faith," why do Islamic scholars, propagators of Islamic faith, leaders, teachers, mothers and fathers restrain "believing youths . . . whose hearts are burning with a fire," who live in the hope that their "pure blood may irrigate the earth"?[37] Teachers do not prevent young people from pursuing their studies in infidel countries "where temptation crashes around him like waves and the oceans of inflamed desires are astir."[38] And yet they discourage jihad. Azzam dismisses the argument that what Afghanistan needs is money not men.[39] He is contemptuous of the wealthy Muslims of the *umma* who think they have fulfilled their obligation "with scraps from their tables and crumbs from their food."[40] The Afghan people say: "The presence of one Arab among us is more loved by us than one million dollars."[41]

In *The Defence of the Muslim Lands* Azzam writes of the five million Afghans who have fled their country, of the seven million who have scattered to the mountains, of the one and a half million who have been martyred. While the countries of the Warsaw Pact devastate Afghanistan, the *umma* quibbles over the difference between *fard kifaya* and *fard ayn.*[42] In *Join the Caravan* he argues that even now, nine years after the invasion, most Muslims "have not heeded the call." "In the ears of the Muslims is a silence rather than the cries of anguish, the screams of the virgins, the wails of the orphan and the sighs of old men."[43]

Jihad is not for Azzam merely an obligation. It is at the heart of his religion. The Prophet himself, he tells us, was involved in twenty-seven military operations and fought in nine. His companions were "bathed in jihad and cleansed of engrossment in worldly matters."[44] Azzam tells the story of a medieval jihadist who killed a thousand Turks with his sword. He would have liked the sword to have been buried with him if that had not been *bidah*, a religious innovation. Azzam tells a Kipling-like story, with the ethnicities reversed, of the Egyptian "butcher" of the English at the Suez Canal, executed by Nasser "to please his American masters."

Jihad is not, however, mere military heroics. Without jihad, lands regained will, once more, easily be lost. With jihad, petty concerns "fall away" and death becomes "a paltry matter." Jihad alone is the only way the glory of the *umma*, the Muslim nation, can be reborn. "Birth cannot be accomplished without labor, and with labor there must be pain."[45] But the meaning of jihad goes even deeper than this. Like Sayyid Qutb, from whose work, as he once wrote, his "worldview" was shaped, so with Azzam, jihad is "the most excellent form of worship" and the highest act of faith.[46] Azzam's words soar to the heavens. "The popular Jihad movement with its long path of effort, great sacrifice and serious effort, purifies souls so that they tower above the lower material world. ... Malice disappears and souls are sharpened; and the caravan moves on up from the foot of the mountain to the lofty summit."[47]

Jihad produces martyrs. In one of his most famous lectures Azzam describes martyrs as the "building block of nations." From a minuscule group of students at Kabul University—"the cream of the cream of the cream"—the great jihad in Afghanistan had been born. Some believed the earth "had been drained of the thirst for martyrdom." This group had proved them wrong. Qutb found his vanguard in a handful of young Muslims in a Cairo apartment separating themselves from society to form a movement so that Islam might be reborn. Azzam found his vanguard in fourteen Afghan students who had sacrificed their lives initiating the struggle against the Soviet invaders of their land. These students had changed the course of history. "The Jihad initially began as a few drops of blood, until Allah decided to ignite the sparks with this blessed people and explode the Jihad, blessing with it the land of Afghanistan and the rest of the Muslims until its good encompassed the whole world." History was written with the blood of the martyrs in the cause of Islam. Without martyrdom and its heavenly rewards, the permanent war against the infidel imagined by the Salafi jihadists could never have been fought. It was Azzam more than any other who placed martyrdom at the center of the ideology that led eventually to the Islamic State.[48]

Abdullah Azzam's place in the evolution of Salafi jihadism is complex. As Muhammad Haniff Hassan, author of *The Father of Jihad*, points out, in certain respects Azzam was more "restrained" than some of his Salafi jihadist contemporaries. He did support the assassination of communist and other infidel leaders. Unlike Faraj and his followers, however, he was opposed to the assassination of Muslim leaders unless authoritative religious opinion had been gathered and a fatwa published. (Somewhat inconsistently, as Hassan also points out, despite these reservations he did offer praise for Sadat's assassin, Khalid al-Islambouli. Perhaps Sadat's signing of a peace treaty with Israel in 1979 made him an exception.)

Azzam did support the killing of Muslims who worked for or supported the communists in Afghanistan. He was, however, seriously concerned about the killing of Muslims in the internecine struggles in Afghanistan he witnessed, which he regarded as sinful. Azzam also opposed, at least in principle, the taking of the lives of women, children, and the aged, forbidden according to the Islamic legal tradition, but defended the killing of women who supported the communists in Afghanistan. While he did support the use of explosive vehicles and vests, in which soldiers lost their lives, as a weapon of war, the question of those "martyrdom operations" targeting civilians, including Muslims—which would become a critical weapon in the arsenal of the Salafi jihadists from the 1990s—did not arise during the course of the Afghan war.[49]

Finally, despite his enthusiastic support for terrorism as a method of waging jihad, Azzam did on occasion write critically about the ruthless ethic he had observed among those whom Hassan calls the "youths on the battlefield more militant than him."[50] "In Islam," Azzam argued, "ends do not justify means; Islam disputes Machiavelli's idea (ends justify means) or Lenin's idea (for the sake of benefit, do whatever you wish) ..."[51] Although, according to Mustafa Hamid, Azzam did support the small number of Saudis who took up arms against the Shi'a

Hazara after their arrival in Afghanistan, as we have seen, Azzam was tolerant of the differences and shortcomings in the religious or cultural practices of the Sunni Muslims he fought alongside in Afghanistan. Unlike later Salafi jihadists, with regard to Sunnis he was no *takfiri*. In these cases he retained an older Islamic sensibility more weakly found in the leaders of al-Qaeda and altogether inconceivable in the leaders of the Islamic State.

Despite these elements of restraint, Abdullah Azzam's influence is fundamental to the evolution of the Salafi jihadist ideology in a number of ways. During the war against the Soviet Army, tens of thousands of young Muslims traveled to Afghanistan to wage jihad.[52] Without Azzam this was unlikely to have occurred. In turn, during the war in Afghanistan, Salafi jihadism was transformed from a vision, as it had been with Qutb, or an underground revolutionary movement, as it had been with Faraj, into the ideology of a global army. With Qutb, the revolutionary imagination of Salafi jihadism had centered on the entire Islamic nation, the *umma*, but as a virtual reality rather than as a political strategy for the really existing contemporary world. With Faraj, the revolutionary mission of Salafi jihadism was grounded in the real world but remained within the boundaries of Egypt, a single nation-state. With Azzam, Salafi jihadism was involved in a protracted war with a real-world enemy fought by an alliance of Afghans and foreign Muslim fighters. In *The Defence of the Muslim Lands*, Azzam argued: "Unfortunately, when we think about Islam we think nationally. We fail to let our vision pass beyond geographic borders that have been drawn up for us by the kuffar."[53] On the Afghan battlefield, that began to change. During the war in Afghanistan and after, in both imagination and revolutionary strategy, the nation-state was gradually replaced for the Salafi jihadists by the *umma*. By the time of 9/11 and the ascendancy of al-Qaeda, Salafi jihadism had become a genuinely global revolutionary movement that had transcended the imaginative and strategic boundary of the nation-state. That process had begun with Azzam and in Afghanistan. In an interview with *Al Jazeera*, Osama bin Laden explained Azzam's influence like this: "When the Sheikh started out, the atmosphere among the Islamists . . . was limited, location-specific, and regional, each dealing with their own particular locale, but he inspired the Islamic movement and motivated Muslims to the broader jihad."[54]

In Afghanistan there were further important developments in the ideology of Salafi jihadism. As many scholars have argued, it was there that Egyptians from a radical Muslim Brotherhood background came into contact with Saudis brought up in the tradition of Wahhabi Salafism. From this contact a chemical reaction in the sphere of ideology occurred which changed the character of both Egyptian Muslim Brotherhood jihadism and Saudi Salafi Wahhabism. The Egyptians politicized the Saudis. The Saudis influenced the Egyptians by their puritanism and textual literalism. So far as I can tell, there have been no detailed studies focusing on this process of Egyptian–Saudi interaction. However, there have been many incisive, although often rather different, descriptions. "When they came in contact with the Muslim Brothers," Bernard Rougier, for example, argues, "the Wahhabi salafists . . . familiarized themselves with the political questions emphasized by the Brotherhood. . . . For their part, the Brothers may have been influenced . . . by the additional legitimacy afforded by the [Wahhabi Salafists'] mastery of the religious corpus."[55]

Muhammad Haniff Hassan has argued that Azzam realized that if the ruthless jihadists he observed on the battlefield
of Afghanistan "were not curtailed, these youth could bring
detriment to themselves and jihad in Afghanistan."[56] Mustafa
Hamid, who fought in Afghanistan and who was an acquaintance of Azzam's and a friend of Osama bin Laden's, was of a
similar opinion. As we have seen, Hamid believes that following
bin Laden's military disaster at Jalalabad in July 1989, where his
reputation was temporarily eclipsed, and the death of Azzam
five months later, when his counterbalancing influence ended,
the ruthlessness of these youths was, indeed, unleashed. Hamid
labels this tendency the Jalalabad School. He regards the aston-
ishingly brutal behavior of both the Salafi jihadists in Algeria in
the mid-1990s and of Zarqawi and his movement in Iraq after
2003 as a consequence.[57] In any explanation of how the mind
of the Islamic State was shaped, the eyewitness accounts of
both Azzam and Hamid, two jihadist fighters—concerning the
emergence of a new ultra-extremist tendency among the Salafi
jihadists on the battlefield in Afghanistan—are compelling.

CHAPTER 5

KNIGHTS UNDER THE PROPHET'S BANNER— OSAMA BIN LADEN AND AYMAN AL-ZAWAHIRI

Two fundamental changes took place in the evolution of Salafi jihadism during the 1990s. The first was the replacement of the Soviet Union by the United States and Israel—the Crusader–Jewish alliance—as the principal enemy of Islam. The second was the development and sanctification of a tactic by which the Crusader–Jewish alliance could be attacked with some prospect of success—suicide bombings targeting not only soldiers but also civilians, known by the Salafi jihadists as "martyrdom operations." The two most consequential Salafi jihadists in the decade following the Soviet withdrawal from Afghanistan were the leader of al-Qaeda, Osama bin Laden, and the Egyptian jihadist revolutionary Ayman al-Zawahiri, the head of al-Jihad from 1991. Bin Laden was chiefly responsible for making the Crusader–Jewish alliance the primary target of the Salafi jihadist movement; Zawahiri for providing the theological justification for martyrdom operations. As Fawaz Gerges argues, this involved two apparent conversions. By the end of the 1990s, Zawahiri accepted bin Laden's strategy that targeted the far enemy and not the near enemy. For his part, bin Laden joined Zawahiri in accepting the legality of killing Muslims, women, and children by bombings involving suicide, both in apparent contravention of long-standing Islamic legal rulings.[1]

During the latter part of the 1980s, relations between the Salafi jihadists and the Saudi regime and its scholars were in general amicable. The Saudi sheikh Abd al-Aziz ibn Baz had offered his support for Abdullah Azzam's fatwa, *The Defence of the Muslim Lands*.[2] A vast amount of money had flowed from Saudi sources to the mujahidin. Osama bin Laden had played the role of intermediary between these Saudi financiers and Azzam. However, when Osama bin Laden returned to Saudi Arabia following the catastrophic Battle of Jalalabad and the withdrawal of Soviet troops from Afghanistan, his relations with the Saudi regime and its religious establishment deteriorated rapidly. The reason was what was called in the Middle East the Second Gulf War.[3]

In August 1990 Saddam Hussein's Iraq invaded and occupied Kuwait. Saudi Arabia was possibly under threat. Bin Laden offered to supply 100,000 jihadi troops to drive Iraq out of Kuwait. Not surprisingly, on behalf of the Saudi regime, its foreign minister, Prince Turki, declined what he clearly regarded as a harebrained scheme. The Saudis supported instead a military mission led by the United States and endorsed by the United Nations, and offered their territory as the base for the American forces.[4]

For bin Laden, the deployment of American troops in the land of the two holy cities, Mecca and Medina, was a turning point. He became a bitter enemy of the apostate Saudi regime and its spineless clerisy, led by ibn Baz, who he argued were willing to produce fatwas of the most egregious kind at the will of their masters—blessing the American troop presence on the holy soil of the Arabian Peninsula and, later, even the Saudi recognition, following the Oslo Accords, of Israel, the Jewish state at the heart of Islam. Rather than remain silent or capitulate to the regime, in May 1991 bin Laden went into exile. He based himself and al-Qaeda in Sudan, the Islamic state established under the moderate Muslim Brother Hassan al-Turabi, taking occasional trips to Pakistan and Afghanistan to support the Taliban in its struggles against the communist government and its Islamic rivals. In 1994 bin Laden established an office in London, "the Advice and Reform Committee," to publicize his anti-Saudi and anti-American position. The Saudis now canceled his citizenship, withdrew his passport, and froze his assets. Bin Laden claimed there were several attempts to arrest or assassinate him. Eventually, in 1996, under intense pressure from the Americans and the Saudis, Turabi offered bin Laden a choice: either shut his mouth or find another home. Bin Laden returned to what he called "the pure and free air" of Afghanistan, living in a cave with his family "high in the peaks of the Hindu Kush." Shortly after, the Taliban entered Kabul.[5]

Osama bin Laden's view of America at this time can be followed by his edicts, interviews, and fatwas, collected by Bruce Lawrence in *Messages to the World*. Although the United States had been invited to the Arabian Peninsula by the Saudi regime, bin Laden regarded the military base the Americans established in Saudi Arabia as an invasion as clear-cut as the Soviet Army's entry into Afghanistan in 1979. Apparently it now filled for him the political and the affective space left empty after the Soviet withdrawal from Afghanistan. He described the American invasion of Saudi Arabia, however, as "a calamity unprecedented in the history of the *umma*"; it was for him far more terrible than the Soviet invasion of Afghanistan.

The United States had invaded the Arabian Peninsula—the lands of Mecca and Medina—which the Prophet had argued must be cleansed of Christians and Jews. Bin Laden regarded the US as the most evil imperial power in the history of humankind. When he spoke about America's recent crimes, apart from its invasion of Saudi Arabia, invariably he listed their support for the Jewish murderers of the Palestinians; the starvation of 600,000 and then one million Iraqi children as a result of the sanctions regime maintained against Iraq; and the atomic attacks on Hiroshima and Nagasaki which killed hundreds of thousands of innocent men, women, and children. Bin Laden regarded Americans not only as wicked but also as hypocrites. Despite their massive crimes—"deeds which you would not find the most ravenous animals debasing themselves to do"— they labeled the mujahidin "terrorists." Their troops were also cowards. The Arab Afghan mujahidin, who saw them run away at the first sign of trouble in Somalia in 1993, thought their "low spiritual morale" compared unfavorably with the tough Soviet troops they had encountered in Afghanistan. Although bin Laden believed the Americans were controlled by the Jews, since the collapse of the Soviet Union the sole remaining superpower acted as if it were "a Master of this world." He thought the ambition of the Americans was nothing less than "to get rid of Islam itself." In an interview for CNN, which took place in March 1997 in the Hindu Kush, bin Laden told the New

Zealand journalist Peter Arnett that even to hear the name Bill Clinton filled him with "disgust and revulsion."[6]

Despite this scathing assessment of the American empire and the danger it represented to Islam, bin Laden's recommendation about how the Americans should be fought radicalized only gradually during the second half of the 1990s. In August 1996, shortly after arriving in Afghanistan, he called for a jihad "against the Judeo-Christian alliance."[7] In March 1997 he told Peter Arnett that he held American civilians "responsible" for the actions of their government "because they chose this government and voted for it" and warned they should leave the lands of Islam at once. However, he also made it clear that the jihad he had announced did not target American civilians, only their soldiers.[8] On February 23, 1998, this changed. In a fatwa by a group that called itself the World Islamic Front, bin Laden and three other signatories called upon all Muslims "to kill the Americans and seize their money wherever and whenever they find them." It advised Muslims that "to kill the Americans and their allies—civilians and military—is an individual duty (*fard ayn*) incumbent upon every Muslim in all countries, in order to liberate the al-Aqsa Mosque and the Holy Mosque."[9]

There have been two explanations of bin Laden's declaration of total war against the Crusader–Jewish alliance at this time. Fawaz Gerges argues that Osama bin Laden was attempting to save the "sinking jihadi ship" that had recently suffered major defeats in both Algeria and Egypt.[10] Mustafa Hamid argues rather differently that having observed the astonishing bloodshed the ultra-extremist Salafi jihadist Armed Islamic Group had visited upon the Algerian civilian population, bin Laden wanted to divert the energies of his young followers toward a war against the Americans and the Jews in order to avoid the Algerianization of the struggle against the apostate regime in Saudi Arabia.[11]

One of the four signatories of this fatwa was the head of al-Jihad, Ayman al-Zawahiri. For some two decades he had been committed to the "near enemy" strategy first outlined by Muhammad Faraj, which gave priority to the struggle against the *taghut* regime in Egypt rather than the final struggle against the far enemy—Israel and its imperial patron, the United States. Indeed, as recently as April 1995, as we have seen, Zawahiri had argued in the magazine *Al-Mujahidin* that "the road to Jerusalem passes through Cairo."[12] Zawahiri's conversion to bin Laden's "far enemy" strategy happened very rapidly, causing consternation within his movement. Perhaps Zawahiri was converted because of the blow inflicted on the jihadists when Egyptian public opinion turned against them after the Luxor terrorist incident of November 1997. Perhaps it occurred, as some have suggested, because of al-Jihad's financial troubles, which only support from bin Laden could remedy.[13] Whatever his reason, one thing is certain: Zawahiri's conversion to bin Laden's "far enemy" strategy and to war against the Crusader–Jewish alliance—which was completed by the merger of al-Jihad and al-Qaeda in mid-2001—was of genuine significance in the history of Salafi jihadism.

The joint bin Laden–Zawahiri fatwa of February 1998 was a prelude to "three strikes" delivered to the United States in the following three years—the bombing of the United States embassies in Kenya and Tanzania on August 7, 1998; the attack on USS *Cole* in Aden on October 12, 2000; and the aircraft attacks on the Twin Towers and the Pentagon on September 11, 2001. All of these actions were suicide bombings or martyrdom operations. Although as recently as November 1996 bin Laden had claimed proudly that the fighting of the mujahidin throughout the war in Afghanistan "was unstained with any blood of innocent people," in the case of the bombings of the African embassies, and of course of 9/11, very many innocent lives were taken.[14] Bin Laden's conversion to martyrdom operations involved two elements that sat uneasily with traditional Islamic jurisprudence: suicide and the killing of Muslims and women and children. It signaled acceptance of the tactic inside Salafi jihadism which al-Jihad had employed in recent years and for which Zawahiri had provided one of the most detailed legal justifications.

In the first half of the 1990s, al-Jihad, alongside its rival and associate al-Gama'a al-Islamiyya, had conducted many suicide bombings inside Egypt, a tactic Zawahiri described as "flea and dog" operations.[15] On August 1993, in reprisal for the arrest of 800 of its members, it targeted the interior minister of Egypt, Hassan Al Alfi, with a "booby-trapped motorcycle." The operation was unsuccessful. Shortly after, in November 1993, al-Jihad made an attempt on the life of the Egyptian prime minister, Atef Sedki. It, too, failed but killed more than twenty bystanders, including a twelve-year-old schoolgirl, Shaima Abdel-Halim. Egyptian public opinion was outraged. In the autumn of 1995, al-Jihad successfully bombed the Egyptian embassy in Islamabad. All of these operations involved suicide. Some involved civilian casualties.[16] Perhaps as a result, at some time in the 1990s (the exact date is uncertain) an advisory legal treatise, "Jihad and the Superiority of Martyrdom," was published under Zawahiri's supervision, examining, from the perspective of Islamic law, suicide bombings and the unintentional killing, during jihad, of Muslims, women, and children.

In Zawahiri's treatise on martyrdom operations and the killing of formerly protected categories, the argument begins with three assertions. The most effective weapon of war is "deceit." Martyrdom in the service of the faith is the most glorious of deaths. When the Muslims waged jihad they were "the mightiest of people" and when they abandoned it "Allah humiliated them through division and conquest." There is, however, something that calls into question the legality of martyrdom operations: the unambiguous verse in the Qur'an forbidding suicide and threatening those who take their own lives with eternal torment in hell. Is there any way to surmount this barrier? In Zawahiri's treatise, an authenticated hadith is quoted concerning a pious young man who advised the king how to take his life so that people would be drawn to the faith. The story of an early medieval scholar, Ibn Kathir, is also quoted, in which 600 warriors at the Battle of Acre sank their boat and drowned to prevent its weapons and provisions falling into the hands of a Crusader, Richard the Lionheart. Numerous other tales about Muslim warriors who lost their lives in circumstances where they knew that death was certain are recounted. Most of the stories concern certain death at others' hands. As a consequence, the treatise is required to argue that there is no difference "between a man killing himself with his own hands or through the agency of another." Martyrdom operations in the waging of jihad and individual suicide both involve a person taking their own life by their own hands. As a consequence, the treatise distinguishes sharply between these two apparently similar styles of death on the basis of "intention." If the death is driven by "depression and despair"—suicide—it guarantees a future of eternal torment in hell. If the purpose of the death is "to serve Islam"—martyrdom—it promises a wondrous future in the highest chamber of heaven.

It is clear, however, that martyrdom operations might involve the killing of Muslims, which the Qur'an expressly and solemnly forbids, and also of women, children, and *dhimmis* (non-Muslims paying tax), whose lives the Prophet made clear ought not to be taken. According to Zawahiri's treatise, the relevant scholarly authorities are divided on the question of the "bombardments" that took place in the age of the Prophet, which risked killing the protected categories of human beings. One school thinks such deaths are totally prohibited. Another believes that in the course of jihad they are always legitimate so long as "blood money" is paid and "atonement" is offered. A third argues that bombardment of "idolaters" is permitted even when they are "intermingled" with protected people, so long as the need is real. The treatise opts for the third school of thought.

The reasons are surprisingly pragmatic. Such tactics are vital, it argues, because the enemies of the mujahidin possess "massive and vigilant armies" making it "next to impossible to confront them in open warfare." In Egypt, Algeria, Palestine, and Lebanon, the "explosives and missiles" used in martyrdom operations have already proven to be remarkably successful. As the enemy deliberately place "their organizations and military escorts" among civilian populations, the taking of the lives of Muslims, women, and children is unfortunately unavoidable. If possible, such people should be protected. But this protection should never be at the expense of waging jihad. If the protected categories are killed, the mujahidin should offer atonement. Blood money should, however, only be paid if it can be afforded. Muslims who are killed as the collateral damage of martyrdom operations can anyhow console themselves with the thought that they too will have died as martyrs. And "as for those dubious persons who say that jihad should be abandoned for now due to certain ambiguities," the Zawahiri treatise concludes, "let them know that forfeiting the faith is a much greater harm than forfeiting money or lives."[17]

It is difficult to exaggerate the importance of Zawahiri's treatise, and of others like it, in the history of Salafi jihadism. In the figure of the jihadist suicide bomber, the warrior is fused with the martyr in a way that licenses a new form of attack. Even the most brutal Salafi jihadists rely on jurisprudential justifications for their acts. In the long term, the justifications of martyrdom operations taking the lives of Muslims and innocent civilians opened the legal-moral floodgates for Zarqawi and other Islamist groups following the 2003 American invasion and occupation of Iraq. More martyrdom operations were conducted in the subsequent four years than in the history of all suicide bombings in all countries since the tactic was introduced in 1981, most importantly during the civil wars in Lebanon and Sri Lanka.[18] In the short term, when Zawahiri's formal defense of martyrdom operations was combined with bin Laden's strategic conception that priority had to be given to the war against the far enemy, both the legal justification and strategic rationale for the 9/11 attacks on the Twin Towers and the Pentagon—which between them bin Laden and Zawahiri planned—were complete.

Shortly after 9/11, Ayman al-Zawahiri wrote *Knights under the Prophet's Banner,* one of the most significant books in the Salafi jihadist canon. *Knights* is a book of many parts—an autobiography; an insider's history of the Salafi jihadist movement in Egypt; a polemic aimed at the Muslim Brothers and the recent nonviolent tendency of a part of al-Gama'a al-Islamiyya; a sweeping geopolitical analysis of the state of the world since the arrival of American troops in the Middle East in 1990; and a wide-ranging plan for jihadist action in the future. When writing *Knights,* Zawahiri was in hiding with a $25 million reward on his head.[19] Unsurprisingly, it reads as if it were his final testament. Although Zawahiri generally refers to his comrades-in-arms as the Islamic movement, in one passage he calls the movement to which he has belonged since his teenage years "the Salafi jihadi current."[20]

Zawahiri begins with an analysis of the significance for Salafi jihadism of Afghanistan—which he first visited as a physician in 1980 and where he returned on many occasions between 1986 and 2001. Although he concedes he once regarded Afghanistan merely "as a secure base" for preparing "jihadist action in Egypt," he recognizes now that the struggle of the mujahidin was fundamental to the development of the Salafi jihadist movement. In Afghanistan, mujahidin from around the world became acquainted with each other, turning jihadism into an international movement fighting on several fronts. In Afghanistan, unlike in Palestine, the resistance movement was untainted by secular currents. In Afghanistan, the myth of the invincible superpower crumbled. Zawahiri denies the American claim that the mujahidin were "obsessed half-mad people" whom they controlled and financed. If they were indeed "mercenaries," why could they not now be bought back? The Americans saw Afghanistan as "a proxy war" against the Soviet Union. The mujahidin turned Afghanistan instead into "a call to revive the neglected religious duty, namely jihad in the cause of God." Afghanistan was thus a dress rehearsal for the present war between the Crusader–Jewish alliance and Islam.[21]

Knights under the Prophet's Banner turns from Afghanistan to a detailed history of the jihadist movement in Egypt, written from the perspective of a major player. Zawahiri insists the movement began in 1966 with the execution of Sayyid Qutb. Qutb is for him unquestionably the preeminent theoretician of the Islamic movement. Not only did Qutb provide the ideological spark that ignited the Salafi jihadi movement. Before Qutb, the Muslim Brothers regarded the enemy as Western imperialism. After him, many jihadists, beginning with Faraj, recognized that their primary enemy was the internal *taghut jahili* regime. This understanding had led to thirty-six years of uninterrupted bloody combat.[22]

The key moment in this struggle was the assassination of Sadat and the courageous defenses of the act offered in the courts of law by the assassin Khalid al-Islambouli and "the scholar of the mujahidin," Sheikh Omar Abdel-Rahman, which exposed to the world the un-Islamic nature of the apostate Sadat regime.[23] Following Sadat's assassination, Zawahiri was imprisoned for three years. According to one persistent story, under torture he betrayed a close comrade.[24] Not surprisingly, therefore, he writes passionately of the increased brutality of the repression following Sadat's assassination. "The brutal treadmill of torture broke bones, stripped out skins, shocked nerves, and killed souls. ... It detained women, committed sexual assaults, and called men feminine names."[25] However, the struggle against the near enemy, inspired by Qutb, operationalized by Faraj, had not ended. Nor, of course, had the repression. Zawahiri documents the violent struggles of both al-Jihad and the rival and associate group al-Gama'a al-Islamiyya, which had been provoked into violence by the Mubarak regime. At the time of writing *Knights*, Zawahiri estimated that there were 60,000 political detainees in Egyptian jails.[26]

In *Knights*, Zawahiri offers a balance sheet of the successes and failures, strengths and weaknesses, of the Egyptian Salafi jihadist movement. They have educated the young, who now grasp the "supremacy of the sharia and the apostasy of their rulers." They have maintained their struggle against the regime over a quarter century—from the Military Technological Academy affair of 1974 to the Luxor attack of 1997—despite the intensity of the repression. Too often, however, their actions have been haphazard and rash. As a movement of elites and specialists, their message is not yet sufficiently grasped by the Muslim masses.[27]

The jihadists have also been betrayed. The Muslim Brothers have now altogether abandoned jihad and begun to participate in the parliamentary game. In 1987 they acknowledged the legitimacy of the *taghut* Mubarak. More recently, they argued that even though the president of Egypt must be a Muslim, there was no reason why its prime minister might not be a Christian. Perhaps, Zawahiri suggests sarcastically, they would consider a Jew. The Muslim Brothers might have grown organizationally in recent years but they have committed ideological and political suicide. Zawahiri traces the root of the Muslim Brothers' collapse to its beloved and sanctified founder, Hassan al-Banna, who was assassinated by an agent of the monarch in 1949. He points out that al-Banna argued, for example, that if there were faults in the constitution they could later be corrected by legislation. So, even al-Banna did not grasp that the constitution of a Muslim was the sharia and that sovereignty belonged to God and not to Man. Certain jihadists were shocked by his harsh criticism of al-Banna in a previous book, *Bitter Harvest.* He answers in these words: "Muslims judge men by righteousness, not righteousness by men."[28] Zawahiri is even more pained by the most recent betrayal. He devotes a large section of *Knights* to a denunciation of the 1997 Tora prison agreement, in which some leaders of al-Gama'a al-Islamiyya agreed to abandon violence and lay down their arms. Their capitulation, Zawahiri argues, "will only instill despair in the hearts of the Muslim youth," which, he adds, is "the cornerstone of the policy of Jewish expansion in the region."[29]

The most important purpose of *Knights under the Prophet's Banner* is to explain to the Salafi jihadists why, after having followed Faraj's strategy of placing priority on the struggle against the near enemy for the past twenty years, Zawahiri now regarded jihad against the far enemy the more urgent strategic priority. This involves an elaborate piece of historical analysis—the unearthing of a sinister, 200-year Crusader plan for the destruction of Islam, which centered on the creation of a Jewish state at the heart of the Middle East.

The first evidence of the plan came to light, according to Zawahiri, when Napoleon claimed that the Jews were "the legitimate heirs to Palestine." More than half a century later, with money borrowed from the Jewish Rothschild bankers, the Jewish prime minister of Britain, Benjamin Disraeli, purchased the Suez Canal. It provided "a golden opportunity for Britain to establish a foothold in Egypt in preparation for establishing Israel." Not long after, in 1877, Jews began settling in Palestine, at Petah Tikva. In World War I, in service of the Jews, the British diplomat Mark Sykes and his French counterpart François Georges-Picot, agreed on a plan for the carving up of the Ottoman Empire. This opened the way for Arthur Balfour's 1917 declaration of Palestine as the Jewish homeland. Shortly after, the *taghut* ruler, King Hussein bin Ali of Saudi Arabia, embraced the idea. The creation of Israel was now a fait accompli. In 1973 Israel was in danger. Only an American airlift saved it. In 1979 Sadat signed a humiliating peace treaty with Israel. It was underwritten by a no less humiliating agreement with the United States, by which Egypt effectively ceded its sovereignty. Israel now went on the rampage. Its first act was the destruction of Iraq's nuclear facility in 1980.

Before 1990 the only military presence in the Middle East America thought it needed was Israel, "a huge US military base." However, with the revival of Islam in Afghanistan and Chechnya and the emergence of the international army of the mujahidin, the United States decided it could no longer rely on its clients in the Middle East and control events "from behind a veil." The result was the dispatch of a huge military force to Saudi Arabia. For Zawahiri this decision was the turning point, as it was for Osama bin Laden, although for somewhat different reasons. Zawahiri was convinced the Americans and the Jews would "not allow any Muslim force to reach power in the Arab countries." He was also convinced that if a Muslim society appeared a possibility in Egypt, the United States would immediately mount an invasion following the route taken by the Napoleonic armies 200 years earlier. "Confining the battle to the domestic enemy" in this new geopolitical situation was therefore no longer "feasible." The ultimate battle between Islam and the far enemy could no longer be postponed.[30]

Apart from God's grace, the greatest asset on the side of Islam in that apparently unequal war was the global army that had emerged from the crucible of Afghanistan—"the youth who have abandoned their families, country, wealth, studies and jobs in search of jihad."[31] Zawahiri gave these mujahidin their marching orders. "Tracking down the Americans and the Jews," he pointed out, "is not impossible." Their aim must be to kill them "with a single bullet, a stab or a device made up of a popular mixture, [even] hitting them with an iron bar." With nothing more than such "available means," the actions of "small groups could prove to be a frightening horror."[32] Zawahiri also recommended striking at Americans and Jews in Muslim countries. Soon, they would "trade accusations" with their *taghut* agents over the question of responsibility and would face a clear choice: outright war with the forces of Islam or a reconsideration of their violent and brutal plans. Either choice would benefit the mujahidin.[33] Zawahiri recommended that the battle should be waged primarily by "martyrdom operations." They were "the most successful way of inflicting damage against the opponent and the least costly to the mujahidin in terms of casualties."[34]

All of this would, however, be "mere and repeated disturbance," he advised, unless land at the heart of Islam was eventually won and held. This Islamic state would in turn provide the base from which "the caliphate based on the traditions of the Prophet" could be restored. Finally, Zawahiri warned the mujahidin against impatience. The creation of an Islamic state and the restoration of the caliphate would most likely be the work of several generations.[35]

In *Knights under the Prophet's Banner,* Zawahiri argued that by 2001 one of the greatest assets of the Islamic movement was the fact that it had "largely succeeded in clarifying the main elements of its ideology, relying on strong evidence from the Qur'an, the Prophet's tradition, and the respected scholars. This provided it with a solid base on which it hoisted its banner."[36] Zawahiri was right. A clear ideology was one of the most powerful weapons of his movement. Thirty-five years after the execution of Sayyid Qutb, a new political ideology—Salafi jihadism—had crystallized. Its main elements, at the time of 9/11, took the following form.

The ideology began with the dark vision of the world Sayyid Qutb had implanted in the imagination of his followers. Since the golden age of the Prophet Muhammad, his companions and followers in the next three generations, the entire world had gradually descended into the same state of ignorance, *jahil-*

iyya, of the polytheist, pagan Arab tribes before the arrival of Islam. This state of ignorance was of course found among the People of the Book—Christians and Jews, who had rejected the message of the final Prophet—and also among the followers of the two principal contemporary secular-materialist political ideologies, capitalism and communism. But its shadow had spread much further, reaching all of the tyrannical and apostate rulers of the world's supposedly Islamic regimes.

This state of near-universal ignorance was, according to Salafi jihadists, a tragedy for humankind. Islam was the one and only religion of truth. Its restoration now relied upon a tiny revolutionary vanguard who understood the faith. In the age of *jahiliyya*, jihad had become, as Faraj taught, the neglected duty. Apart from faith itself, jihad was in fact a Muslim's highest duty. Jihad had to be waged to restore true Islam to the supposedly Muslim world and to the lands the Muslims had lost during the long era of their decline, and then at long last to bring the blessings of Islam to the infidel, *kuffar*, world in its entirety. The meaning of all of this could not have been clearer. The resurrection of humankind from the era of near-universal *jahiliyya* rested on the success of the jihadist struggles of the Islamic vanguard. The *umma* would be built of the blood and limbs and corpses of the jihadis. Of all deaths, most glorious was the death of the martyr.

Despite the darkness of its vision of the present and its embrace of extreme violence, Salafi jihadism was an unambiguously utopian ideology. What it aimed to create was a world where the Oneness of God, *tawhid*—monotheism is too thin and abstract a translation—was acknowledged by all peoples of the earth. All innovations (*bidah*) in Islam that had corrupted the faith since the golden age of Mecca and Medina had to be rejected. So had all of the fundamental political convictions and institutions of the contemporary world. A single Islamic world community, the *umma*, had to triumph over the nation-state, the grotesque formation that had divided human beings since the Treaty of Westphalia, and replace that collectivity of grotesqueries, the United Nations. Sovereignty, *hakimiyya*, in the *umma* had to rest exclusively with God. Democracy, which represented the sovereignty of the people rather than the sovereignty of God, was an obscenity and an impertinence. The shape of life in the *umma* and its law were to be based exclusively on the sharia, found in the Qur'an. Laws made by men in parliaments or elsewhere were an abomination. The punishments set out in the Qur'an, the *huddud*, had to be strictly enforced *à la lettre*. The Qur'an and the accounts of the life and sayings of the Prophet, as recorded in the authentic hadiths, contained almost everything that humans needed to know about how societies should be formed and how men and women should live. Only where there existed doubts might there be a need to consult the most reliable religious authorities, like the Salafi jihadists' favorites, the medieval scholar Ibn Taymiyya and his disciples.

The ideology of Salafi jihadism also contained a tragic version of history. Once, Islam had represented the most glorious and powerful civilization, expanding its message over the Middle East, Central Asia, North Africa, and parts of Europe, including Spain. As the true faith was corrupted and forgotten, Islam had descended into its present state of abjection and humiliation. In the essentialized historical imagination of the Salafi jihadists—in which the base motives and vicious characters of whole categories of people remained unchanged despite the passing of several centuries—the alliance of the Crusaders (the Christian West) and the Jews was the most enduring and dangerous enemy of Islam.

As Zawahiri had explained, at the end of World War I, in the interest of their long-standing plan to impose a Jewish state in the heart of Islam, the Crusaders had carved the Ottoman Empire into a series of colonial states, in a process encoded in the ideology as the "Sykes–Picot conspiracy." At the end of World War II, they had completed their most heinous crime and inflicted the most painful wound, the creation of Israel. Salafi jihadists argued that the Jews controlled one of the postwar superpowers, the United States. Since Faraj and Azzam (who followed the lead of Hassan al-Banna) the Salafi jihadists had distinguished between collective responsibility, *fard kifaya*, for offensive jihad to expand the faith, and individual responsibility, *fard ayn*, for defensive jihad when the *umma* was under threat. In 1979 Afghanistan had been invaded by the Soviet Union. In 1990 the Middle East had been invaded by the Crusaders. Once again, therefore, jihad had become the unavoidable duty of every Muslim man and woman.

Since Faraj, the Salafi jihadists had been divided over the question of whether the struggle against the Crusader–Jewish alliance should first be waged against the near enemy or the far enemy. Most opted at first for the near enemy. When, however, Saudi Arabia invited the Americans to station their forces in the land of the two holiest Muslim sites and cities, the balance of the ideology shifted. In 1998 the most important Salafi jihadist movement of that time, Osama bin Laden's al-Qaeda, published a fatwa calling for jihad against the far enemy and for its followers to kill Americans and Jews whenever and wherever the opportunity arose. The principal method it advocated in the asymmetrical war it declared—between the Crusader–Jewish alliance and Islam—was the martyrdom operation, involving the apparently forbidden act of suicide and the killing of formerly protected categories of people, sanctified in the advisory treatise written under the supervision of Zawahiri.

Al-Qaeda's overwhelmingly most significant success was 9/11, the surprise attack on the Pentagon and the Twin Towers, with 3,000 murdered. According to the ideology, the task that now awaited the true Muslims was to create an Islamic state. That Islamic state would prepare the way in the longer term for the restoration of the caliphate. Once the caliphate was restored, war against the infidel would be waged until all of the lands of infidelity—not only the formerly Islamic lands that had been lost—finally embraced the one and only true faith.

The emergence of a genuinely new and significant ideology is one of the rarest events in political history. Salafi jihadism is the most recent example. Although it had crystallized by the time of 9/11, until the arrival of Zarqawi and the creation of the Islamic State its evolution into its most fully and startlingly brutal form was not complete. Many milestones had been passed. But Salafi jihadism had not yet reached the gates of hell.

CHAPTER 6

THE MANAGEMENT OF SAVAGERY— ABU BAKR NAJI AND ABU MUS'AB AL-ZARQAWI

Both before and after 9/11, according to his writings collected in *Messages to the World* and the recollections of fellow jihadist Mustafa Hamid, Osama bin Laden believed it only a matter of time before the great enemy of the *umma*, the United States, would experience catastrophe.[1] Bin Laden had witnessed the disintegration of the Soviet Union shortly after its withdrawal from Afghanistan. It was now "a figment of imagination." He attributed its defeat to the courageous armed struggle of the mujahidin behind which stood the blessing and the guiding hand of God. Bin Laden was convinced that the Soviet Union had been a far more formidable superpower than the United States. He believed that America was the most decadent culture in human history, obsessed by the pursuit of wealth and luxury, corrupted by a depth of moral licentiousness never before seen. He believed that the myth of American power had now been exposed to the world by nineteen devout and courageous Muslim student martyrs. The greatest buildings of the empire had fallen. Wall Street had been paralyzed by panic. The fig leaf of human rights had been abandoned.

Bin Laden was contemptuous of the argument put by the "gang of criminals in the White House whose idiotic leader claims that we despise their way of life." The action had been mounted because the Americans and Jews had believed they could inflict untold misery on the *umma* without fear of reprisal, or even any concern that the world would take notice of its suffering. Finally, with 9/11, "the balance of terror" had to some extent been "evened out." In fear of further strikes on their own soil, Americans, he hoped, would now find life "an insupportable hell."

Following 9/11, bin Laden believed, the greatest Crusade in history had been mounted. In reprisal for an action that had cost the mujahidin a paltry half a million dollars, the United States had spent a trillion dollars or more, first invading Afghanistan and then, in March 2003, Iraq. Afghanistan had been invaded to destroy the threat posed by the Taliban, who had created the world's only true Islamic state. Bin Laden was certain, however, that the ultimate Crusader ambition was to take control of the entire Middle East—in part because it wanted the "black gold" on which the prosperity of the American empire relied; more deeply in pursuit of total victory in the "clash of civilizations" between Islam and the West, history's final drama. The victory of one civilization would bring darkness to humankind. The victory of the other would bring liberation and light.

Bin Laden claimed to have personally witnessed how the Americans' airpower had been incapable of overwhelming the Muslims in the Battle of Tora Bora in Afghanistan in December 2001. By 2003 he was immensely encouraged by the quagmire the Americans had sunk into after their invasion of Iraq, "screaming at the top of its voice as it falls apart in front of the whole world." He was certain that Islam would emerge victorious. God willed this victory. Moreover, at "the pinnacle" of Islam was the stipulation: "You fight, so you exist." Yet how exactly the victory of the mujahidin was to be achieved was far from clear. Nine months after the American invasion of Iraq, in an interview with *Al Jazeera* called "Resist the New Rome," the best strategy for victory bin Laden could come up with was establishing a "temporary council" of notable Muslims in a "safe haven" with a popularly selected "imam," ruling according to "the book of God and the tradition of the Prophets." The council, he advised, should arm the people with light weaponry in preparation for a "general mobilization" so that "the raid of the Romans, which started in Iraq" might, God willing, be "repulsed."[2]

This was, to put it mildly, a hopelessly vague suggestion. The explanation of how the American invasion of Iraq might be used to bring the Islamic State to birth relied on the writings of other, more systematic, Salafi jihadist thinkers.

The Management of Savagery: The Most Critical Stage through which the Umma Will Pass was published online in 2004 under the *nom de révolution* Abu Bakr Naji. Its author is believed to be the Egyptian Muhammad Khalil al-Hakim, who had written a previous work, *The Myth of Delusion: Exposing the American Intelligence*, published on September 11, 2001.[3] Some of *Management* appears to have been written before and some after 9/11, with a small section added after the invasion of Iraq. In part it is military-cum-political-science, in part history, in part theology. The argument is intricate and occasionally arcane; the style sometimes forensic, sometimes poetic, sometimes prophetic. Many serious scholars of Salafi jihadism regard it as a vital source of inspiration in the creation of the Islamic State. Its translator, the American William McCants, describes it as a "blueprint."[4]

The argument begins with an analysis of the geopolitical situation following World War II, when the Soviet Union and the United States took control of the world, forcing almost all countries to orbit around one superpower or the other. The superpowers dominated through their wealth and weaponry, and through their pretense to both invincibility and benevolence, which Naji describes as their "deceptive media halo."[5] The Soviet Union had now collapsed. Its prolonged and costly war in Afghanistan against the mujahidin had exposed the fraudulence of its media halo and the sources of internal vulnerability, like the spiritual death found in a materialist society and the danger it faced by relying on the distribution of "worldly pleasures" as its sole source of legitimacy.[6]

Since 9/11, the situation of the other superpower, the United States, had become similarly parlous. By invading Afghanistan and Iraq, the United States had fallen into the trap set for it by the mujahidin. It was in danger of "military overstretch," just as the American historian Paul Kennedy, who is cited, once warned it would be. The United States was even more vulnerable than the Soviet Union was in the 1980s. As a consequence of its cultural decadence, its soldiers were "effeminate." As a consequence of its geographical distance from the Middle East, the wars it was fighting against the Muslims were more difficult and ruinously expensive.[7]

The Americans' media halo, first exposed by the "miracle" of 9/11, would soon be utterly discredited and the hatred of the slumbering Muslim masses finally aroused.[8] Moreover, as America lurched from one crisis to another, the helplessness and vulnerability of the Muslim client *taghut* regimes in its orbit would become increasingly obvious. When America was forced to withdraw from Iraq, as it assuredly would be, "the terror which will be in [their] hearts ... will be indescribable." The *umma* must grasp this historic opportunity. If the moment passed, "generations of Muslims will be lost in the mire of having to submit to *taghut* courts of law and will drown in televised carnal appetites."[9] "If not now," Naji asks, "then when?"[10]

The Management of Savagery is a systematic exposition of what the mujahidin must now do so as not to squander the unique opportunity offered by 9/11 and the invasion of Iraq. Naji acknowledges that the mujahidin are presently only at the very beginning of their work. Research undertaken before 9/11 by another Salafi jihadist grand strategist, Abu Mus'ab al-Suri, suggested that the most promising regions for activity were Jordan, North Africa, Nigeria, Pakistan, and the Gulf states.[11] The invasions of Afghanistan and Iraq had shown that other opportunities might suddenly arise. Where central power exists more or less intact, the mujahidin should involve themselves in what Naji calls "vexation and exhaustion" operations whose aim is the creation of mayhem or savage chaos.[12] Where central power is nonexistent or weak—as it was in Afghanistan following the Soviet withdrawal, and as it most likely will be in many other regions of opportunity as American power melts away—the condition of savage chaos already prevails or shortly will.

Naji's book is principally an attempt to explain to the mujahidin how they can mount vexation and exhaustion operations to create regions of savage chaos; how they can then take control and manage the regions of savagery that have emerged; and how, from the consolidation of different regions of managed savagery, the next historic stage—the stage of the construction of Islamic states—can be accomplished. His vision does not stop at this point. Eventually, all of the lands once Muslim—"Jerusalem, Bukhara, Samarkand, Andalusia"—must be restored to Islam. Only then will the mujahidin begin on their final, most vital task of "liberating the earth and humanity from the hegemony of unbelief and tyranny through the power of God."[13]

The heart of Naji's treatise is his explanation of the military and political strategy and tactics by which the mujahidin can take the first step in this "long journey . . . of limbs, blood and corpses" to create and then manage savagery.[14] Almost uniquely in the Salafi jihadist canon, Naji warns the mujahidin that, if they are to succeed, a grasp of political science is vital. A "political map" of the mind of the Crusader enemy is no less important than a "military map" of the region where battle is to be joined. Naji explains that despite their pretense to "religious" or "cultural" motives, the Crusaders are driven almost exclusively by base materialism, the desire for "an unruffled life of comfort and luxury." Everything is therefore subordinate to self-interest—"friendship or enmity; peace or war." The Crusaders believe that there are no eternal friendships, only eternal interests, and that politics is "the art of the possible." As a result, as soon as they strike trouble, even solemn agreements with coalition partners will begin to crumble. "Only when they think their opponent is weak and it is possible to crush his will" will they persist "in continuing war."[15]

The present era is primarily one of vexation and exhaustion operations against the *taghut* regimes or the Crusaders. Naji praises as exemplary the Bali operation which took the lives of so many Australian tourists. He recommends at this stage of history attacks on not only tourist resorts but also "usurious" banks or famous apostate authors.[16] Such attacks will spread a more generalized fear in hundreds of similar sites or among corresponding human types. He is particularly enthusiastic about attacks mounted against the petroleum industry in the Middle East. These will force the enemy to concentrate its most loyal troops around oil fields and installations, leaving the remaining small numbers of soldiers isolated in peripheral regions increasingly vulnerable and therefore, through fear, "forced to choose between killing or joining us, or fleeing and abandoning their weapons."[17] Once more, an understanding of politics is critical. Naji is very concerned that the mujahidin explain their actions and justify their consequences—the economic costs and the enemy's counterattacks—with rational arguments and sharia texts through plausible audio and video productions which appeal to the masses, not only the elites. Quite unusually, Naji fully grasps the vital role played by the mass media under contemporary conditions of war.[18]

What is perhaps most chilling about *The Management of Savagery* are the very many passages explaining forensically the political logic behind the infliction of extreme violence on the enemy. An explosion targeting a building must be of such ferocity that "the earth completely swallows it up."[19] During the battles, hostages will be taken. "If the demands are not met, the hostages should be liquidated in a terrifying manner." On occasion, spies in the mujahidin's ranks will be uncovered.

Even the lowliest must be killed "with the utmost coarseness and ugliness."[20] Here, the friend of the Prophet, Abu Bakr, the most merciful of souls, is his great inspiration. Naji reminds his readers three times that Abu Bakr punished a traitor by burning him alive. One order he issued to his army "dealt only with the matter of severing the neck without clemency."[21] For Naji, one of the vital methods for the conduct of the battle by the mujahidin is what he calls "paying the price."[22] Following each enemy action, there must be retribution in at least equal measure, preferably in an unexpected region, even if it takes years before it is able to be carried out. The enemy must know that every time it kills members of the mujahidin forces "vengeance for our blood will be undertaken" according to the principle "blood for blood and destruction for destruction."[23]

None of this violence is random or meaningless. Its simple purpose is to "fill the enemy's hearts with fear" and to leave them with feelings of "hopelessness."[24] But there is another, more complex political end. As the war progresses, one of the most important ambitions of the mujahidin is to "polarize" society into two camps: the followers of falsity and the followers of truth. By making "this battle very violent, such that death is a heartbeat away," people will come to realize that they must choose between one kind of death promising paradise and another promising hell. On this earth, however, the political ambition of the mujahidin is to use extreme violence to create conditions of savage chaos. In such conditions, people yearn for security, above all else. As the mujahidin gradually gain the upper hand over the Crusaders and their *taghut* client regimes, people will flock to them because of their strength.[25]

As news of their victories spreads, the best potential recruits for jihad—"exuberant" youth in whom the human instinct is still most alive—will migrate from distant regions to join the jihadist caravan.[26] They will need to learn from their elders whom they can rightly target—avoiding, on the one hand, the zealotry that tarnished the image of the mujahidin during the Algerian Civil War, who embraced the principle "everyone who is not with us is against us," and, on the other, the destructive humanitarianism of "the person of exaggerated erudition" who deplores the spilling of blood.[27] Spies will be needed to penetrate the ranks of the army, police, and political parties of the apostate enemy.[28] Best suited for this work are those elite among the youthful mujahidin who can "fend off intellectual doubts and bodily desires."[29]

Not all youth are suited for jihad. Those already hardened in battle know that war "is naught but violence, crudeness, terrorism and massacring." Naji is gravely concerned and, indeed, scathing about the gentleness of the contemporary Muslim character. "The Arabs used to fight and know the nature of war." Many no longer do. "It is better for those who have the intention to begin a jihadi action and are also soft to sit in their homes."[30] The mujahidin must be able not only to inflict but also to endure extreme violence. Naji tells the story of an Afghan who was unmoved by the screaming of a child of his own family who had just witnessed an unspeakable horror. An Arab asked him, "Have you no feeling?" The Afghan replied: "This is war, and you and I will die like them one day."[31] This Afghan is Naji's idea of the exemplary mujahidin, of the exemplary human being. He believes the corrupt spirit of the *taghut* regimes renders them incapable of sustaining a long war. To avoid this, they will resort to mass arrests, hellish imprisonments, and torture of their enemies. This is of political advantage to the mujahidin. Nothing better prepares young men for brutal killing than hatred for their torturers.[32]

With God's grace, the mujahidin will triumph in their wars against the Crusaders and their *taghut* clients. They already are. One of the most exalted passages in *The Management of Savagery* concerns the progress of the mujahidin's war against the occupiers of Iraq. The American soldiers have proven themselves to be cowardly and incompetent. Naji has even read newspaper reports of "epilepsy and madness" among them. God has shown his favor to the mujahidin by visiting upon the American troops a series of miraculous pestilences: "massive spiders ... which spread terror in their hearts" and "mosquitoes ... which cause the skin to swell and collapse, for which there is no cure." He has also sent ghostly apparitions, fighting on the side of the mujahidin, which even "the advanced weaponry of the Americans could not harm."[33]

If the Muslims now wish to create the Islamic State, they must recognize the fundamental lesson of history: that all states, not merely Islamic ones, "are established after oceans of blood."[34] This is not for Naji in the slightest a melancholy or regrettable truth. Jihad "completely refashions the personality." It alone provides the condition in which the human spirit is tested and perfected and where "altruism becomes easy and egotism falls away." Even more deeply, only by participating in the most violent struggles will the eyes of the individual be opened to the beauty of Islam. As Sayyid Qutb understood, the Qur'an delivers its secrets only to those whose frame of mind has been shaped in battle. Trials and tribulations "remove the darkness from the eyes and the dust from the heart." "Terrible events and the steadfastness of human exemplars in the face of the horrors firmly root ideas which could not be taught to people in hundreds of years of peaceful education."[35] Naji contrasts the most admirable human being, the battle-hardened mujahidin, to the contemptible Muslim man of peace who "cannot imagine himself outside his air-conditioned mosque or outside his office under the fans."[36]

The most startling section of *The Management of Savagery* comes at its conclusion, in the chapter entitled "Our Method Is a Mercy to All Beings." At the time of Noah's flood, God destroyed all unbelievers. In the early days of Islam, the sword of God smote Arab polytheists, unconverted Jews and Christians, Muslims who sinned against the faith, apostates who abandoned their religion. Jihad is, however, not merely an expression of God's stern justice. "Despite the blood, corpses and limbs which encompass the killing and fighting which its practice entails," jihad, Naji tells us, is God's "greatest mercy to man."[37] In George Orwell's imagined totalitarian state, "War is Peace" and "Slavery is Freedom." In Abu Bakr Naji's blood-soaked *The Management of Savagery*, "Slaughter is Mercy."

Someone, perhaps Talleyrand, once wrote of a political event: "It was worse than a crime, it was a mistake." This aphorism might have been coined for the American-led invasion of Iraq of March 2003. The disintegration of the brutal Iraqi regime of Saddam Hussein provided the opportunity for the Salafi jihadist movement to mount its greatest vexation and exhaustion operation thus far in history. Eventually it came to be led by Abu Musab al-Zarqawi, the spiritual father of the Islamic State.

Zarqawi was a Jordanian from a poor Bedouin family who graduated from a life of violent petty crime to jihadist Islam in his early twenties. In 1989 he traveled to Afghanistan, but too late to participate in the anti-Soviet war. In 1992 he became a student of one of the influential and doctrinally extreme Salafi jihadists, Abu Muhammad al-Maqdisi. Zarqawi and Maqdisi returned to Jordan and shortly after were imprisoned together. The gentle, scholarly Maqdisi ceded leadership of their prison followers to his far tougher and more charismatic pupil. Zarqawi suffered prolonged torture. It appears to have had the kind of effect on him that Naji described.

As soon as he was released from prison under the royal amnesty of 1999, Zarqawi quit Jordan for Afghanistan. Having met Osama bin Laden there, he established his own jihadist training camp at Herat, close to the Iranian border. The camp was independent of al-Qaeda but had a friendly relationship with it. Here, Zarqawi fell under the influence of an even more extreme Salafi jihadist theological scholar than Maqdisi, Abu Abdullah al-Muhajir, who taught at the ultra-radical Khaldan camp, which recruited new mujahidin in rivalry with al-Qaeda.

Following 9/11 and the US attack on Afghanistan, Zarqawi fled with his principally Palestinian, Jordanian, Syrian, and Lebanese followers first to Pakistan and then to Iran, before entering the Kurdish areas of Iraq shortly before the by now generally expected American invasion. Kurdish intelligence alerted the Americans to his presence. In his pre-invasion address to the United Nations on February 3, 2003, the US secretary of state, Colin Powell, argued that Zarqawi had links with Saddam Hussein and was an agent of al-Qaeda. Both claims were entirely false.

When Zarqawi entered Iraq, he called his group of some thirty mujahidin Jama'at al-Tawhid wal-Jihad. In *The Management of Savagery*, perhaps coincidentally, the phrase "the people of *tawhid* and jihad" occurs repeatedly. Within two years or so, Zarqawi's fighters numbered in the thousands. According to Zarqawi, by January 2004 Jama'at al-Tawhid wal-Jihad had conducted twenty-five operations, and had been responsible for some of Iraq's most notorious acts of terror, beginning in August 2003 with the bombing in Baghdad of the Jordanian embassy and the headquarters of the United Nations. Zarqawi targeted especially Shi'a marketplaces and holy sites. In April 2004, American Nicholas Berg was publicly beheaded, probably by Zarqawi in person. The film of his execution was then distributed widely. In February 2006 Zarqawi's men destroyed the dome of the al-Askari mosque, one of the Shi'a Muslims' most holy sites, in the central Iraqi city of Samarra.[38]

Zarqawi was clearly inspired in this campaign by the strategic and tactical theory of *The Management of Savagery*. Michael Weiss and Hassan Hassan, the authors of *ISIS: Inside the Army of Terror*, learned that it circulated very widely among the Islamic State's "commanders" and its "rank-and-file fighters."[39] Even more revealing, in the first history of the creation of the Islamic State, published shortly after its foundation, the intellectual debt Zarqawi owed to Naji is made unmistakably clear.

Shaykh Abu Mus'ab [Zarqawi] . . . strived to create as much chaos as possible. . . . With chaos, he intended to prevent any taghut regime from ever achieving a degree of stability. . . . He would order to carry out *nikayah* [injury] operations dozens of times in a dozen areas daily, targeting and killing sometimes hundreds of apostates from the police forces and

Rafidah. .... These attacks [would] compel apostate forces to partially withdraw from rural territory and regroup in major urban regions. The *jama'ah* [group] would then take advantage of the situation by increasing the chaos to a point of leading to the complete collapse of the *taghut* regime in entire areas, a situation some refer to as "*tawahhush*" ("mayhem"). The next step would be to fill the vacuum ... [with] a full-fledged state.[40]

This is Naji in a nutshell. Even though Zarqawi and his successors do not mention *The Management of Savagery* as their inspiration, this passage comes very close. The Arabic title of *The Management of Savagery* is *Idarat at-Tawahhush.*

In two articles from mid-2004, and later in an interview with *Al Jazeera*, Zarqawi's first mentor, Maqdisi, questioned the ferocity of the campaign that was being waged by the mujahidin in Iraq. Zarqawi was leading the youth into "an inferno." The "bright image" of jihad was being distorted by "car bombings, roadside bombs, and throwing mortars and the like on public streets and markets etc." "Beware," he warned Zarqawi, "of leniency in what we are commonly stern about regarding the sanctity of Muslim blood, livelihood and honor."[41] As Maqdisi was one of Salafi jihadism's most prominent and respected jurisprudential scholars, the public reprimand he delivered to his most famous former student needed to be answered. Zarqawi's response, written in a tone of more-in-sorrow-than-in-anger, was published on June 21, 2005. He tells of a mutual friend who wept when he saw the pain that Maqdisi's criticism had caused. He points out that from his prison cell in Jordan Maqdisi is incapable of understanding the situation on the ground. Zarqawi reminds Maqdisi that there is a difference between a mentor and a slave. Only toward the end of his response is there a sense of threat. Zarqawi informs Maqdisi that copies of his *Al Jazeera* article are being circulated widely by the enemies of Islam in Iraq, "the cross worshippers, secularists, Rafidah, the Islamic Party and all other deviant groups." If the enemies of the jihad in Iraq are victorious, "I can assure you, Abu Muhammad, that in terms of who gets credit . . . you will walk away with the lion's share." It is, however, not too late for Maqdisi to repent.

In the course of his rebuttal, Zarqawi mentions something of which he believes Maqdisi might be unaware. Maqdisi is by no means his only or even his most important mentor. It is true, he concedes, that when they were together in Afghanistan in the early 1990s he was totally opposed to martyrdom operations. However, when he returned to Afghanistan in 1999 he had encountered a Salafi jihadist who, in a brilliant article, had convinced him that on that question he was wrong. Zarqawi had invited this man to present a ten-day workshop in his Herat training camp, "to explain the legality of those operations to the brothers there." His explanation had a "very positive impact." Zarqawi names his new mentor—Sheikh Abu Abdullah Al-Muhajir, the author of a famous work, *Issues in the Jurisprudence of Jihad*, known among the mujahidin as *The Jurisprudence of the Blood.*[42]

To understand the mind of the Islamic State—the radicalization it underwent in the transition from Osama bin Laden and Ayman al-Zawahiri to Abu Mus'ab al-Zaqarwi—it is vital to grasp the influence of the theology of Muhajir on Zarqawi.

THE MIND OF THE ISLAMIC STATE

Mayssara al-Gharib was Zarqawi's media spokesman in Iraq. He has written about Zarqawi's profound love and reverence for Muhajir. According to Gharib, Zarqawi urged him to teach their followers from a photocopy of Muhajir's *The Pioneers of Spreading the Sunnah in the Hallmarks of the Victorious Sect*. When, during the second battle of Fallujah, a copy of *The Jurisprudence of the Blood* finally arrived, Zarqawi's followers were overjoyed.[43]

In *The "Islamic State" Organization*, published in Jordan, the scholars Hassan Abu Hanieh and Mohammad Abu Rumman provide a useful summary of Muhajir's jurisprudence. According to Muhajir, all countries in the world are part of *Dar al-Harb*, the Abode of War. In this abode, Muslims are "allowed to desecrate the blood and property of infidels as they please." The killings can continue "until no infidel remains" on earth. Martyrdom operations are regarded as permissible "without the slightest doubt." Nor is there the slightest doubt about "beheading infidel fighters, and slitting their throats." As Muhajir points out, in their jihad against "the enemies of God," Muslims have practiced beheadings and throat slittings "generation after generation, from the time of the Prophets until this day." There are no methods of killing that are impermissible. Muhajir points out that "the Mujahideen worshippers of God" are permitted "to attack, kill and fight the belligerent infidels in every means that would take their lives and extract their souls from their bodies in order to cleanse the earth from their filth." In the case of defensive wars—and all wars being fought by the mujahidin today are by definition defensive—"we find it permissible to attack belligerent infidels, kill and fight them ... even if the means [are] what are known today as Weapons of Mass Destruction, including nuclear, chemical, biological and so forth."[44]

The Management of Savagery provided Zarqawi with the tactical and strategic rationale for his startlingly brutal behavior. *The Jurisprudence of the Blood* provided him with its theological justification. If the mind of the Islamic State is to be understood, the impact on Zarqawi of the teachings of Naji and Muharjir are of critical importance.

Zarqawi was a man of action not of words. There exists, however, one fascinating lengthy letter from him to the leaders of al-Qaeda, dated January 2004. Its purpose was in part to outline the strategic situation from the point of view of a frontline mujahidin fighter and in part to begin what turned out to be a protracted negotiation for Jama'at al-Tawhid wal-Jihad's entry into al-Qaeda. In this letter, the future character of the Islamic State can be foreseen.

Zarqawi begins within an apocalyptic frame. In Sham (the ancient name for Iraq and Syria) "the decisive battle between the infidels and Islam is taking place." As al-Qaeda no doubt already grasps, he continues, the Zionist-led American administration of George W. Bush entered Iraq under "a contract to create the State of Greater Israel from the Nile to the Euphrates." Their purpose was "to hasten the arrival of the Messiah." What is the political situation following the invasion? The Kurds, in whom faith has died, "have given themselves heart and soul to the Americans" and have "opened their lands to the Jews." The Sunni Muslim masses are in a desperate state. "More helpless than orphans at the table of the despised ... they have lost their leader" and are wandering in the desert "divided and dispersed." The Muslim Brothers, one of their political parties, "trade in the blood of martyrs" and change sides "according to the way the wind is blowing." One source of their religious leadership, the Sufi sheikhs, "sing and dance under the leadership of a camel driver." Even the timid Iraqi mujahidin are a grave disappointment. "Uneducated and inexperienced," they have no political "vision" and do not grasp the central truth— that "safety and victory are incompatible," that power cannot be attained "without dipping into blood and facing death."

The treachery of the Kurds and the weakness of the Sunnis does not, however, constitute what Zarqawi regards as the greatest internal problem the mujahidin face following the American occupation. Their overwhelming problem is the evil enemy of the Sunnis, the Shi'ites. It is difficult to convey the depth of hatred for the Shi'a Zarqawi's letter reveals. They are "the most vile people in the human race," "the insurmountable obstacle, the prowling serpent, the crafty evil scorpion, the enemy lying in wait." Throughout history, the Shi'a have stabbed the Muslims in the back. As the medieval scholar Ibn Taymiyya understood, they served the Mongols when they subjugated Islam. When Islam stood at the gates of Vienna, Shi'a treachery at home forced the Muslim armies to retreat. Now they have allied with the Americans in their grasp for power. Their ultimate ambition is to create a great Shi'a state including Iraq, Iran, Syria, and Lebanon. They cunningly hide their true nature with "honeyed" words, "exploiting the naiveté and goodness of the Sunnis." Their religion "has nothing in common with Islam." Perhaps worst of all, throughout history they have served the interests of the Jews.

What then is to be done? Zarqawi is convinced that the

Americans do not pose a long-term danger. "The battle we are waging [against the Americans] is an easy matter. We consider it a certainty that the Crusader will disappear in short order." The key, according to Zarqawi, is to provoke a Sunni–Shi'a civil war. "We will trigger their rage against the Sunnis ... [forcing them] to bare their fangs. ... If we manage to draw them onto the terrain of partisan war ... soon the [Sunni] sleepers will awaken from their leaden slumber." Prospects in this struggle are bright. "The Shi'ites are a nation of traitors and cowards." Once aroused, the Sunnis will fight. Zarqawi concludes his letter by asking the leaders of al-Qaeda whether they accept his plan. If they do, he promises, they will have his allegiance.[45]

Bin Laden and Zawahiri must have faced a difficult decision in pondering future relations with Zarqawi. On the one hand, the ferocious battle Zarqawi was leading in Iraq was the most promising ever mounted by the Salafi jihadist movement. On the other, the war against the Shi'a Zarqawi was intent on fighting represented a radical break in the history of the mujahidin. Clearly, either admiration for Zarqawi or a judgment of the political advantages of alignment with him, or most likely both, overcame concern. In December 2004 al-Qaeda accepted the formal allegiance (*bay'at*) Zarqawi offered. Jama'at al-Tawhid wal-Jihad became al-Qaeda in the Land of the Two Rivers. Even though it was not yet the largest movement among the Iraqi Salafi jihadists, Osama bin Laden requested all groups of Iraqi mujahidin recognize Zarqawi as their leader. At the conclusion of the negotiations, Zarqawi published a brash commentary making it clear that in the "eight-month" negotiation he, and not al-Qaeda, had been the victor. "Points of view were exchanged, and a fateful disconnect occurred, but God soon blessed us with the return of communications, whereby our noble brothers in 'Al-Qaeda' came to understand the strategy of the 'Al-Tawhid wa al-Jihad' group in the land of Mesopotamia . . . and their hearts were open to our approach there."[46]

In July 2005 another long letter was dispatched from al-Qaeda Central to al-Qaeda in the Land of the Two Rivers. All scholars say that this letter was sent directly to Zarqawi from Zawahiri. This cannot be right. Toward its conclusion it reads: "By God, if by chance you're going to Fallujah, send greetings to Abu Mus'ab al-Zarqawi." Most likely, its contents were intended for Zarqawi, but it was sent via another al-Qaeda member. The letter documents al-Qaeda's ambivalence about their new supporter. Zawahiri begins by offering Zarqawi's movement his congratulations, his regret that hiding in Waziristan he is unable to travel to Iraq to join the jihad, and his acknowledgment that those in the heat of battle are better placed to judge military realities than those watching from afar. Despite this, it is not long before Zawahiri, in a rather condescending tone, begins to offer instructions. Al-Qaeda in Iraq must strive to expel the Americans from Iraq, establish an Iraqi emirate (the "piece of land" he had written about in *Knights*), extend the field of battle to neighboring regions, and prepare for war with Israel.

Zawahiri arrives now at a series of harsh and fundamental criticisms of Zarqawi's approach. The battle for the Islamic State cannot succeed without the support of the Muslim masses. They will never accept the disrespect that has been shown for the Sunni religious leaders. Zarqawi and his followers must not think of ruling on the basis of the mujahidin alone. Zawahiri reminds Zarqawi of the isolation the Taliban faced in 2001 following the

American invasion. He must work now to create a broad-based Shura Council, based on the precedent of the golden age.

Even more sternly, Zawahiri chides Zarqawi for his anti-Shi'a sectarianism. No doubt many Shi'a have behaved treacherously during the American occupation. No doubt their understanding of Islam is deeply mistaken. Eventually this will have to be corrected. But the Muslim masses will never understand a program based on the destruction of holy sites or systematic killing, especially of ordinary Shi'a. They will ask: "Can the mujahidin kill all the Shi'a in Iraq? Has any Islamic state in history ever tried that? And why kill ordinary Shi'a considering that they are forgiven because of their ignorance?" Zawahiri continues with a discussion of Zarqawi's public beheading of hostages. They might "sow terror in the hearts of the Crusaders." They might be a means of visiting upon the enemy a little of the suffering they have inflicted. But such scenes will never become "palatable" to the Muslim masses. Zawahiri urges Zarqawi not to be seduced by the praise of the zealous young who have described him as the "sheikh of the slaughterers." He reminds him that captives can be dispatched by a bullet. He ends his letter vaingloriously with news about his many publications, and rather pitifully with a request for $100,000.[47]

Zawahiri's letter was obviously ignored. On September 16, 2005, al-Qaeda in the Land of the Two Rivers announced: "The organization has decided to declare a total war against the Rafidite Shi'ites throughout Iraq."[48] Some three months later, a senior al-Qaeda leader, Atiyatullah al-Libi, sent another, far blunter warning. If Zawahiri's letter concerned Zarqawi's political mistakes, al-Libi's concerned the defects of his character. Although this letter is almost unknown in the scholarly literature, it is even more revealing about the future of the Islamic State than Zawahiri's.

Al-Libi's letter contains a devastating catalogue of the dangers of Zarqawi's style of leadership. Zarqawi is warned he must treat religious leaders with respect. "Address them with utmost kindness ... they are the keys to the Muslim community." He must work with tribal leaders and "try to convince them we are not going over their heads." If religious leaders or tribal leaders are "obeyed or of good repute," on no account are they to be killed. Zarqawi must strive to win the love of the Sunni Muslims. "Do not be harsh with them or degrade them or frighten them." He must learn to accept disagreement. It does "not require hatred, clashing, hostility or enmity." He must not become "arrogant" because of praise. He must show "affection ... and absolute true sympathy" for his inner circle and teach them to avoid "injustice, arrogance, conceit, haughtiness, superciliousness, excessive harshness and violence."

Al-Libi reminds Zarqawi that Islam is a religion of "mercy, justice and good deeds." A balance must be found "between severity and softness, between violence and gentleness." "Let us not merely be people of killing, slaughter, blood, cunning, insult and harshness." Al-Libi had seen such behavior before, from the Algerian mujahidin. "Their enemy did not defeat them but rather they defeated themselves." For al-Qaeda and mainstream Salafi jihadism, but not members of the Jalalabad School like Zarqawi, "Algeria" now symbolizes the road that must not be traveled. Zarqawi is finally warned: "You need to look deeply within yourself and your character." If he fails to heed these warnings, he will be replaced. How the al-Qaeda exiles hiding in Waziristan thought this might be achieved is very far from clear.[49]

It was evident by now that not only through his unrestrained brutality and the expanding circle of what he regarded as permissible under Islamic law, but also in his attitude to the Shi'a, Zarqawi had transformed and radicalized Salafi jihadism. Within the Salafi tradition, there had for a very long time been a highly developed strain of violent anti-Shi'a feeling. This is unsurprising: Salafism is the movement within Islam that reveres the golden age of the Prophet and his companions, and the Shi'a dispute the legitimacy of the first three caliphs. In recent years, scores of books by Salafis have been published and a dozen websites established dedicated to the anti-Shi'a cause.[50] But before Zarqawi the attitudes of the most important Salafi jihadists to the question of what was to be done about the Shi'a were complex. Some, like his second mentor, Muhajir, shared his murderous hatred.[51] Others, like his first mentor, Maqdisi, deplored the Shi'a, but equally deplored their slaughter.[52] As did al-Qaeda. In theory, it was profoundly hostile. Article 23 of its "Creed and Path" reads: "We believe that the rejectionist Shi'a are a group of unbelievers and apostates, and that they consist of the most evil beings under the celestial dome."[53] In practice, however, during the struggles against the Crusader–Jewish alliance, al-Qaeda was willing to postpone the eventual confrontation. As Bernard Haykel points out, in their writings neither bin Laden nor Zawahiri attacked the Shi'a before the invasion of Iraq, and even after it "apparently somewhat reluctantly."[54] It was primarily Zarqawi who brought a genocidal desire to rid the earth of the Shi'a to the center of the Salafi jihadist tradition and the mind of the Islamic State.

Zarqawi was killed by the Americans on June 7, 2006. Shortly after his death, his successors fulfilled his wishes by announcing the existence of the Islamic State of Iraq. On April 17, 2007, its leader, Abu Omar al-Baghdadi, delivered a speech celebrating the new Iraq. He praised the father who killed his own "spy son" and "the women of Iraq [who] shed tears demanding martyrdom operations." His principal theme, however, was that, despite recent setbacks for Muslims in Afghanistan, Bosnia, and the former lands of the Soviet Union, the Islamic State of Iraq would "remain."[55]

This was far from certain. For a time, the warnings al-Libi had issued about the dire political consequences of Zarqawi's brutal behavior seemed accurate. One tribal sheikh from the Sunni Triangle told American researchers a typical story about the troops of the Islamic State of Iraq: "When you went from al Qaim to Ramadi ... you would find tens of bodies without heads alongside the road ... And they forbid anyone to bury them ... The smell was terrible. Ten days later they said ok, it's allowed to bury them, but they left IEDs inside the bodies. When their families went to get the bodies to bury them, they detonated the bomb."[56] Unsurprisingly, the Americans found eager partners among the Sunni tribes in the anti-insurgency movement called the Sahwa, the Awakening. The Islamic State of Iraq was forced to retreat to the arid lands of Al Anbar in the west. In 2008 one of the wives of a leader, Abbu Ayyub al-Masri, inquired, "Where is the Islamic State you're talking about? We're living in the desert."[57]

CHAPTER 7

DABIQ—
THE MIND OF
THE ISLAMIC STATE

T he Islamic State of Iraq (ISI), by now under the leadership of Abu Bakr al-Baghdadi, emerged from the desert in 2011 during the military and political withdrawal of the Americans from Iraq, the increasing persecution of the Sunnis by the government of Nouri al-Maliki, and the descent of Syria into civil war. ISI began taking territory in the Sunni Triangle and dispatched a small force to Syria led by Abu Mohammad al-Julani, which became known as the al-Nusra Front. In April 2013 ISI and the al-Nusra Front fell out speedily, spectacularly, and bloodily after Baghdadi's unilateral announcement of his leadership of a new political entity called the Islamic State of Iraq and al-Sham, covering the lands of both Iraq and Syria. By this time, Osama bin Laden had been killed by the Americans. Al-Qaeda's new leader, Zawahiri, attempted unsuccessfully to arbitrate the differences, requiring Julani to limit his authority to Syria and Baghdadi to Iraq.[1] For his pains, Zawahiri was labeled by Baghdadi an apologist for Sykes–Picot.[2]

In September 2013, Zawahiri published what he called *General Guidelines for Jihad*, an apparent and belated attempt to reassert al-Qaeda's ideological authority over the global Salafi jihadist movement. Zawahiri reminded the mujahidin that their main struggle must be conducted against the far enemy, the Americans, whose weakening grip on power had been revealed by the Arab Spring. Wars against the near enemy ought only to be fought where they could not be avoided or where persecution of Muslims had become unbearable. Fighting against "deviant sects," such as the Shi'a, ought also to be avoided, except in the case of self-defense, and even then only in proportion to the danger posed. Christian, Sikh, and Hindu communities should wherever possible be left in peace, even after the Islamic State was established. The mujahidin should pay respect to scholars. Even "evil" ones should be refuted rather than killed. Their fight was against the Crusader–Jewish alliance and not against fellow Muslims. He warned the mujahadin to "refrain from killing non-combatant women and children ... from harming Muslims by explosions, killing [or] kidnapping ... [and] from targeting enemies in mosques, markets and gatherings where they mix with Muslims or those who do not fight us."[3] Zawahiri's *Guidelines* was an attempt to rescue the Salafi jihadist movement from what he regarded as the grievous strategic, jurisprudential, and sectarian errors introduced into it in Iraq by Zarqawi and his successors. Its publication formalized an ideological division in Salafi jihadism, between ISIS and al-Qaeda, as fundamental as the split that tore the Bolsheviks and the Mensheviks apart in the Second Congress of the Russian Social Democratic Labor Party in 1903.

Zawahiri's appointed mediator between ISIS and the al-Nusra Front and six of his companions were assassinated by ISIS operatives near Aleppo. In February 2014, al-Qaeda severed all links with ISIS.[4] But as so often in radical politics, the momentum was with the extreme. In early June, ISIS conquered Mosul. Controlling considerable territory in the east of Syria and the west of Iraq, on June 29, 2014, it announced that the long-awaited caliphate had been restored. ISIS now styled itself simply the Islamic State.[5]

The Islamic State followed the creation of the caliphate by publishing, almost immediately, an elegant official online magazine in several languages, which it called *Dabiq*. Although no one appears to know who is responsible for its production, its articles are self-evidently written by intellectuals steeped in the theological tradition of Islam, with a deep knowledge of the Qur'an, the hadiths, and major Islamic scholars.[6] Its spirit is murderous and martial. Each issue contains dozens of photographs, many celebrating the dispatching of enemies by knife or bullet, and the great military victories or the successful martyrdom operations of its noble mujahidin. At the time of writing, fifteen issues have appeared, amounting to more than half a million words. Although *Dabiq* is an indispensable source for an understanding of the ideology of the Islamic State, so far as I am aware no systematic analysis of its content yet exists in either the scholarly or popular literature.

Dabiq is heir to the tradition of Salafi jihadism running from Qutb to bin Laden and Zawahiri summarized at the conclusion of chapter 5. Without some grasp of that tradition, it cannot be understood. Yet what is most interesting about *Dabiq* is what it reveals about the changes in both the style and content of Salafi jihadism that have taken place in the years since the Iraq insurgency began. Zarqawi led the Iraq insurgency for only three years. He was not a theorist but a warrior, killed eight years before the declaration of the caliphate. Nonetheless, in a way that is difficult to understand or explain, it is Zarqawi's brutal spirit and worldview that shape the ideology of the Islamic State. Zarqawism, as expressed in the pages of *Dabiq*, represents a new and perhaps final chapter in the ideological history of Salafi jihadism.

The influence of *The Management of Savagery* is still obvious. It was in the history of the caliphate in the opening issue of *Dabiq* that the Islamic State's debt to Naji was first made clear.[7] Later issues congratulate the mujahidin of Libya for the way they have created "mayhem," an ideal condition for jihad, and report the words of a Tunisian supporter of the Islamic State: "We wanted to create chaos."[8] As we have seen, Naji's revolutionary methodology involved the creation of savage chaos through vexation and exhaustion operations destabilizing, destroying, and then filling the power vacuum left by the *taghut* regimes.

The influence of Naji is also obvious in the attitude toward "paying the price," through the kind of exemplary punishments even Zawahiri, one of the architects of 9/11, could not stomach. In *Dabiq* there are scores of examples. Chilling photos are reproduced of the beheadings of captured Crusaders following the decision of the United States and its allies to mount airstrikes against the Islamic State. In Issue 3, we see James Wright Foley grimacing in terror moments before his head is removed.[9] In Issue 4, there is a photo of the severed head of the "Jewish–Crusader" Steven Sotloff, and, as proof of the special perfidy of this dual citizen, another of his Israeli passport.[10] When Shinzō Abe decided to donate $200 million to the war against the Islamic State, Issue 7 published a photo of a Japanese hostage on the point of his execution by beheading. *Dabiq* asks, was Abe so foolish as not to realize that when he made his decision the Islamic State held two Japanese prisoners?[11]

Among those paying the price are the citizens in the countries at war with the Islamic State. On several occasions *Dabiq* has published a passage from the man who was its official spokesman before his death in August 2016, Abu Mohammad al-Adnani: "If you can kill a disbelieving American or European—especially the spiteful and filthy French—or an Australian, or a Canadian, or any other disbeliever from the disbelievers waging wars, including the citizens of the countries that entered into a coalition against the Islamic State, then rely upon Allah, and kill him in any manner."[12] It is extremely enthusiastic about lone wolf attacks. *Dabiq* was delighted about the Sydney siege of Man Haron Monis, in particular because of his eleventh-hour conversion from Shi'ism to Sunni Islam.[13] It was equally delighted by the slaughter in Orlando, because of the choice of victims. "On the 7th of Ramadan," Issue 15 reports, "our brother Omar Mateen, one of the soldiers of the caliphate in America, carried out an attack on a nightclub for sodomites in the city of Orlando, Florida. He succeeded in massacring the filthy Crusaders, killing and injuring more than 100 of them before he was killed."[14] *Dabiq* of course cheered loudly the reprisal operations the Islamic State did plan: the downing of the Russian aircraft after its entry into the Syrian civil war, and the mass shootings in Paris and Belgium.[15] Time and again, it points out that no one should describe these attacks as driven by envy of the Western way of life. They are acts of war. Citizens of countries not involved in the fight against the Islamic State are safe, unless of course one of them insults the Prophet.

Perhaps the most shocking issues of *Dabiq* concerning the "paying the price" punishments are the ones covering the death of captured Jordanian pilot Mu'adh Safi Yusuf al-Kasasibah, who participated in airstrikes against the Islamic State. In Issue 6, Kasasibah is asked in an interview if he knows his fate. "Yes . . . They will kill me."[16] Issue 7 has an article which begins with a large photo showing him being burned alive in a cage and concludes with another of his charred body. The authors admit that in one text the Qur'an seems to make it clear that punishment by burning is forbidden. "None should punish with fire except Allah." Against this, however, they quote another text: "And if you punish [an enemy], punish with an equivalent of that with which you were harmed," as well as several passages from the hadiths involving punishments by burning alive, including those Abu Bakr cited in *The Management of Savagery*. All of this reveals the rather grotesque role played throughout all issues of *Dabiq* by the authors' undoubted scholarly credentials.[17]

The extreme cruelty the victims of the Islamic State experience is announced proudly and is deliberately made conspicuous, unlike the partial cloud of secrecy which surrounded most of the worst crimes perpetrated by the twentieth century's most terrible regimes—those led by Hitler, Stalin, and Pol Pot. In several issues of *Dabiq*, there are photos of the political or religious enemies of the Islamic State, just before or after the moment of their execution.[18] They are described as having been "harvested."[19] The political logic is clear. The fate of the Islamic State's victims is meant to instill paralyzing fear into the hearts of its enemies, as Naji taught that it should. The killing fields are on proud display.

The turn to apocalyptic or eschatological themes is an even

more significant Zarqawist addition to the Salafi jihadist tradition than the ones inspired by *The Management of Savagery*. According to the scholars of Islam, apocalyptic thinking is far more common among Shi'as than Sunnis and far more common on the Arab street than among the educated classes. Although brief apocalyptic references to the Day of Judgment can be found in the writings of bin Laden and Zawahiri, in the words of William McCants, the author of *The ISIS Apocalypse*, they are "languid" rather than "urgent."[20] By contrast, apocalyptic thinking is at the very heart of the Zarqawist version of Salafi jihadism.

Every issue of *Dabiq* begins with his words: "The spark has been lit here in Iraq, and its heat will continue to intensify—by Allah's permission—until it burns the crusader armies in Dabiq."[21] The reference is to one of the Islamic State's most favored apocalyptic hadith, whose first line reads: "The Hour [the Day of Judgment] will not be established until the Romans land at al-A'maq or Dabiq." There are several similar hadiths, whose overall meaning is summarized in Issue 4 of *Dabiq*. The Muslims will be at war with the Romans. There will be a truce. For a time they will fight a common enemy. The Romans will betray the Muslims and raise their cross. This will be followed by the final and bloodiest battle—known as al-Malhamah al-Kubra. The Muslims will be victorious. They will conquer Constantinople and then Rome. Islam will then rule the world.[22] In the mind of the Islamic State the historical moment before the Hour has now arrived, and the war being fought between the Islamic State and the Crusaders will lead to the final battle, in which Islam is certain eventually to prevail.

A frozen mythic past centered on the medieval Crusades

and an imagined future foreseen in the apocalyptic hadiths provide the authors at *Dabiq* with a severely distorted grasp of reality in the present. Let one example suffice. In *Dabiq* there are several passages speculating about the possibility of a "truce" between the Islamic State and the United States, a prospect about as likely as Caliph Abu Bakr al-Baghdadi being awarded the Nobel Prize for Peace. There is only one reason the possibility is discussed. It is mentioned frequently in the favored eschatological hadiths.[23] Zarqawist thinking is drenched in apocalyptic prophecies, frequently occurring in unexpected contexts. As is well known, after conquering Yazidi territories, the Islamic State took women as sexual slaves. For Zarqawists, this is a highly favorable omen. In several obscure apocalyptic texts, the increasing prevalence of slavery is associated with the final battle of history.[24] When Islam defeats "Rome," the leaders of the Islamic State believe American women will be sold in their slave markets. In perhaps the only joke in the thousand pages of *Dabiq*, it is said that Michelle Obama will be lucky if she fetches even one third of a dinar.[25]

The attitude to non-Sunni Muslims is, as we have seen, another major addition Zarqawism has made to the tradition of Salafi jihadism. It is based on two closely connected theological concepts—*wala and bara* and *takfir*. While both *wala and bara* and *takfir* are ideas with a long and complex history, in the worldview of the Islamic State they have become exceedingly, indeed excruciatingly, simple. *Wala and bara* means love of Muslims and hatred of non-Muslims; *takfir*, the belief that the fate of heretics and apostates should be death. The leaders of the Islamic State are frequently described by their Muslim enemies in a single word—*takfiri*.

The Islamic State has also inherited Zarqawi's hatred of Shi'a, as expressed in his letter to bin Laden of January 2004. *Dabiq* has published several long extracts from this letter; it is clearly regarded as a foundational text.[26] *Dabiq* replicates all Zarqawi's claims, time and time again. The Shi'a—who are routinely called by the abusive name *Rafida*—are apostates, polytheists, betrayers of Islam in the past, secret plotters in the present, morally degraded, friends of the Jews, and so on. It adds, however, to the by now familiar catalogue of charges a novel apocalyptic dimension. It has been observed by the authors at *Dabiq* that the Shi'a's Mahdi bears an uncanny resemblance to Dajjal, the Muslim version of the Antichrist, with reddish skin, a big belly, and curly hair, hiding his identity as a Jew.[27] The conclusion they draw is straightforward. "The Rafidah are mushrik apostates who must be killed wherever they are to be found, until no Rafidi walks on the face of the earth."[28]

The Shi'a (and their Syrian branch, the Alawites) are not the only people the Islamic State has destined for death. Issue 4 of *Dabiq* discusses the problem of the Yazidis, the worshippers of the fallen angel Iblis, whose "creed is so deviant from the truth that even cross-worshipping Christians for ages considered them devil worshippers and Satanists." A Qur'anic verse is quoted: "Kill the mushrikin [polytheists] wherever you find them." And a troubling matter of conscience is raised: "Their continual existence to this day is a matter that Muslims should question as they will be asked about it on Judgment Day." Their fate is not in doubt.[29] And not only theirs. Issue 10 of *Dabiq* discusses a recent massacre of Druze villagers by the al-Nusra Front, for which its leaders had apologized. The Druze are described as "worse than the Jews and the Christians." The apology of the al-Nusra Front is mocked: "So ... spilling the blood of the apostate and treacherous Druze is oppression!" And the opinion of Ibn Taymiyya is endorsed: "[The Druze] are to be killed wherever they are found." Without conversion to Islam, all of the Druze must die.[30]

Intentional killing of religious groups in whole or in part is one of the crimes covered by the United Nations Convention for the Prevention and Punishment of the Crime of Genocide. Regarding Shi'as, Alawites, Yazidis, and Druze, and also in reality Christians and Jews, the Islamic State has proudly announced its genocidal intent. The Islamic State does not care two hoots about a United Nations convention. It is, however, sensitive to the charge of Kharijism that Muslims increasingly have laid against it, a very serious accusation in the history of Islam. Kharijism now means, in essence, the fanatical and unjustified condemnation of fellow Muslims as heretics or apostates deserving of death. To refute this rather plausible and therefore damaging accusation, in Issue 6 *Dabiq* announced the discovery of a secret Kharijite cell inside the Islamic State, whose members had pronounced *takfir* on the faithful Sunni masses of Syria and Iraq. The cell was said to be biding their time, waiting for successful enemy attacks, before unleashing their plot to destroy the caliphate.[31] It is the kind of "discovery" Stalin's secret police routinely made.

Sigmund Freud once wrote about "the narcissism of small differences," the exaggerated hostility of people sharing an almost identical worldview. This idea helps explain the relations between the Islamic State and the present leader of al-Qaeda, Ayman al-Zawahiri. The ideological attack on Zawahiri was first mounted systematically in Issue 6 of *Dabiq*, where he is described as the Islamic State's "most ardent opponent."[32] So savage was the attack, *Dabiq* published a clarification in its following issue, making it clear that their deep admiration for Osama bin Laden had not been affected by the sins of his successor and closest collaborator. The attack on Zawahiri intensified in subsequent issues. Zawahiri was accused of "senility" and of "twisted and deviant thinking"; of condoning the al-Nusra Front's disgraceful political coalitions with apostates; of advancing the claims of the lying leader of the Taliban as a counter-caliph; and of showing some sympathy for the despised Egyptian leader of the Muslim Brotherhood, Mohamed Morsi. He was also condemned for his "feeble" and errant *General Guidelines for Jihad,* and for being not a true jihadist but what was scathingly described on several occasions as a "jihad claimant."[33]

More than any other issue, however, it was Zawahiri's opposition to the Zarqawist intention of killing all Shi'as and all members of other supposedly heretical or apostate Muslim sects that finalized the ideological breach between the Islamic State and al-Qaeda. In his *Guidelines,* as we have seen, Zawahiri argues that members of non-Sunni sects should only be killed if they first attack Sunni Muslims. In response, *Dabiq* argued that the fundamental issue between the Islamic State and Zawahiri concerned his grave errors over the question of *takfir.* While Zarqawi rightly "considered the blood of the Rafidah obligatory to kill," Zawahiri refused to take their "filthy blood" and "censured any attempt at reviving jihad against these pagan apostates."[34] In tone and content, this story bears an uncanny resemblance to Soviet politics of the 1930s. Zawahiri was in the process of becoming for the caliph Baghdadi what Trotsky had once been to Stalin.

The mood of the Islamic State has always been triumphalist—recording the joy of the Muslim masses as the liberating army of the Islamic State arrived; celebrating the journey (*hijrah*) of Muslims as they make their way from the lands of infidelity to the land of Islam; cheering each new offer of allegiance from the four corners of the globe; congratulating each new martyr who has found his way to paradise.[35] Its message has also always been profoundly Manichaean. The world is rapidly dividing into two camps: the camp of faith and the camp of unbelief. What the Islamic State calls the "greyzone" between these camps is on the edge of extinction.

The Islamic State recognizes that it has waged war with a world which stretches from President Obama to Ayman al-Zawahiri. As *Dabiq* puts it: "The Islamic State will continue to wage war against the apostates until they repent from apostasy. It will continue to wage war against the pagans until they accept Islam. It will continue to wage war against the Jewish state until the Jews hide behind their gharqad trees [a reference from a hadith]. And it will continue to wage war against the Christians until the truce decreed sometime before the Malhamah."[36] Because of its apocalyptic mind-set, despite the rather formidable number of its enemies, the leaders of the Islamic State believe that in that last great battle for the world before the Day of Judgment, the armies of Islam and the armies of the Christians will do battle in Dabiq, that the Muslim armies will be victorious, and that they will then march upon and conquer Constantinople before raising the flag of Islam over Rome.

As I was about to submit the manuscript of this book, while still reeling from the Islamic State–inspired massacres in the Orlando nightclub, the marketplace in Baghdad, and the promenade in Nice, the fifteenth issue of *Dabiq* arrived over the Internet. A passage from its final page caught my attention:

> The clear difference between Muslims and the corrupt and deviant Jews and Christians is that Muslims are not ashamed of abiding by the rules sent down from their Lord regarding war and enforcement of divine law. So if it were the Muslims, instead of the Crusaders, who had fought the Japanese and Vietnamese or invaded the lands of the Native Americans, there would have been no regrets in killing and enslaving those therein. And since those mujahidin would have done so bound by the Law, they would have been thorough and without some "politically correct" need to apologize years later. The Japanese, for example, would have been force-fully converted to Islam from their pagan ways—and if they stubbornly declined, perhaps another nuke would change their mind. The Vietnamese would likewise be offered Islam or beds of napalm. As for the Native Americans—after the slaughter of their men, those who favor small-pox to surren-dering to their Lord—then the Muslims would have taken their surviving women and children as slaves, raising the chil-dren as model Muslims and impregnating their women to produce a new generation of mujahidin. As for the treach-erous Jews of Europe and elsewhere—those who would betray their covenant—then their post-pubescent males would face a slaughter that would make the Holocaust sound like a bedtime story, as their women would be made to serve their husbands' and their fathers' killers.[37]

Fifty years after Sayyid Qutb's execution, this is what the tradition of Salafi jihadism, the mind of the Islamic State, has become. There are no more milestones to pass. We have finally reached the gates of hell.

NOTES

CHAPTER 1: THE LANDSCAPE OF SALAFI JIHADISM

1. ISIS stands for the Islamic State of Iraq and Syria; ISIL, for the Islamic State of Iraq and the Levant (a Western translation of the idea of al-Sham).

2. Fawaz A. Gerges, *ISIS: A History* (Princeton and Oxford: Princeton University Press, 2016), p. 1. According to Gerges, estimates of the cost of training the Iraqi security forces vary between $8 billion and $25 billion.

3. David Remnick, "Going the Distance," *New Yorker*, January 27, 2014.

4. Robert Manne, "Explaining the Invasion," in *Why the War Was Wrong*, ed. Raimond Gaita (Melbourne: Text Publishing, 2003).

5. Gilles Kepel, *The Roots of Radical Islam* (London: Saqi Books, 2005), p. 41.

6. Ibid., chap. 7.

7. Peter Bergen and Paul Cruickshank, "Revisiting the Early Al Qaeda: An Updated Account of Its Formative Years," *Studies in Conflict & Terrorism* 35 (2016): 1–36.

8. Bruce Lawrence, ed., *Messages to the World: The Statements of Osama bin Laden* (London and New York: Verso, 2005).

9. "Letter Signed by Zarqawi, Seized in Iraq in 2004," in *Zarqawi: The New Face of al-Qaeda*, by Jean-Charles Brisard with Damien Martinez (Cambridge, UK: Polity, 2005), pp. 233–51.

10. Abu Bakr Naji, *The Management of Savagery*, trans. William McCants, for the John M. Olin Institute for Strategic Studies, Harvard University, 2006. Al-Muhajir's work is summarized in Hassan Abu Hanieh and Mohammad Abu Rumman, *The "Islamic State" Organization* (Jordan and Iraq: Friedrich Ebert Stiftung, 2015).

11. Quoted in Hassan Hassan, "The Sectarianism of the Islamic State: Ideological Roots and Political Context," Carnegie Endowment for International Peace, June 13, 2016, p. 14.

12. For example, Christopher Hitchens, "Defending Islamofascism," *Slate*, October 22, 2007.

13. For example, John Gray, "How Marx Turned Muslim," *Independent*, July 27, 2002.

14. For example, Lawrence Davidson, *Islamic Fundamentalism*, 3rd ed. (Santa Barbara, CA: Praeger, 2013).

15. Quintan Wiktorowicz, "Anatomy of the Salafi Movement," *Studies in Conflict & Terrorism* 29 (2006): 207–39.

16. "Dismantling a Khariji Cell," *Dabiq*, no. 6, p. 31.

17. Mustafa Hamid and Leah Farrall, *The Arabs at War in Afghanistan* (London: Hurst, 2015), *passim* but esp. pp. 309–11; 313–14.

18. Joas Wagemakers, *A Quietist Jihadi: The Ideology and Influence of Abu Muhammad al-Maqdisi* (New York: Cambridge University Press, 2012), p. 65.

19. "The Burning of the Murtadd Pilot," *Dabiq*, no. 6, pp. 6–8.

20. "The Rafidah: From Ibn Saba to the Dajjal," *Dabiq*, no. 13, p. 45.

21. For example, "Battle for Fallujah: Mass Grave with 400 Bodies Found in Iraq," *Sydney Morning Herald*, June 6, 2016.

CHAPTER 2: *MILESTONES*—SAYYID QUTB

1. See John Calvert, *Sayyid Qutb and the Origins of Radical Islamism* (New York: Columbia University Press, 2010); Adnan A. Musallam, *From Secularism to Jihad*, Westport, CT, and London: Praeger, 2005); James Toth, *Sayyid Qutb: The Life and Legacy of a Radical Islamic Intellectual* (New York: Oxford University Press, 2013).

2. Calvert, *Sayyid Qutb*, chap. 4; Musallam, *From Secularism to Jihad*, chap. 6; Lawrence Wright, *The Looming Tower: Al-Qaeda's Road to 9/11* (New York: Penguin, 2006), pp. 16–24.

3. Calvert, *Sayyid Qutb*, chaps. 5–6.

4. Ibid., p. 173.

5. Ibid., p. 201.

6. Ibid., chap. 7.

7. Ibid., p. 263.

8. Wright, *Looming Tower*, pp. 36–37.

9. Quintan Wiktorowicz, "A Genealogy of Radical Islam," *Studies in Conflict & Terrorism* 28 (2005): 78–79.

10. William E. Shepard, "Sayyid Qutb's Doctrine of Jahiliyya," *International Journal of Middle Eastern Studies* 35 (2003): 521–45.

11. Sayyid Qutb, *Milestones*, repr. ed. (New Delhi: Islamic Book Service, 2005), p. 7.

12. Ibid., p. 12.

13. Ibid., p. 15.

14. Ibid., pp. 25–29.

15. Ibid., p. 116.

16. Ibid., pp. 47–48.

17. Ibid., pp. 35–36.

18. Ibid., p. 42.

19. Ibid., p. 102.

20. Ibid., p. 137.

21. Ibid., p. 71.

22. Albert J. Bergsten, ed., *The Sayyid Qutb Reader: Selected Writings on Politics, Religion and Society* (New York: Routledge, 2008), esp. 139–41.

23. Qutb, *Milestones*, p. 59.

24. Ibid., chap. 4, "Jihaad in the Cause of God," esp. pp. 72–76.

25. Ibid., p. 62.

26. Ibid., pp. 63–68.

27. Ibid., p. 80.

28. Ibid., pp. 81–82.

29. Ibid., pp. 83–84.

30. Shepard, "Sayyid Qutb's Doctrine of Jahiliyya," esp. pp. 523–25.

31. Qutb, *Milestones*, chap. 6, "The Universal Law."

32. John C. Zimmerman, "Sayyid Qutb's Influence on the September 11 Attacks," *Terrorism and Political Violence* 16, no. 2 (2010): 222–52.

33. Qutb, *Milestones*, chap. 8, "The Islamic Concept and Culture."

34. Ibid., pp. 104–105.

35. Ibid., pp. 97–99.

36. Ibid., chap. 7, "Islam Is the Real Civilization."

37. Olivier Roy, *Globalized Islam: The Search for the New Umma* (London: Hurst, 2004).

38. Qutb, *Milestones*, chap. 9, "A Muslim's Nationality and His Belief," esp. pp. 123–26.

39. Ibid., chap. 10, "Far-Reaching Changes."

40. Ibid., pp. 159–60.

41. Ibid., chap. 11.

42. Ibid., p. 145.

43. See for example Wilfred Cantwell Smith's famous remark: "The fundamental malaise of modern Islam is a sense that something has gone wrong with Islamic history." Quoted in Shepard, "Sayyid Qutb's Doctrine of Jahiliyya," p. 538.

44. Qutb, *Milestones*, chap. 12, "This Is the Road."

45. Zimmerman, "Sayyid Qutb's Influence," p. 222.

46. Calvert, *Sayyid Qutb*, pp. 157–58.

47. Kepel, *Roots of Radical Islam*; Calvert, *Sayyid Qutb*, chap. 8; Musallam, *From Secularism to Jihad*, chap. 8.

48. Muhammad Haniff Hassan, *The Father of Jihad* (London: Imperial College Press, 2014), p. 19.

49. Abdullah Azzam, *Join the Caravan*, accessed at Religioscope online, pt. 1, p. 6.

50. Wright, *Looming Tower*, p. 79.

51. Ayman al-Zawahiri, *Knights under the Prophet's Banner*, in *His Own Words: A Translation of the Writings of Dr. Ayman al Zawahiri*, ed. Laura Mansfield (Old Tappan, NJ: TLG Publications, 2006), p. 48.

52. Calvert, *Sayyid Qutb*, pp. 273–80.

53. Musallam, *From Secularism to Jihad*, p. 117.

54. Kepel, *Roots of Radical Islam*, p. 27.

55. Bergsten, *Sayyid Qutb Reader*, pp. 145–46.

56. Qutb, *Milestones*, p. 150.

57. Calvert, *Sayyid Qutb*, p. 274.

CHAPTER 3: *THE NEGLECTED DUTY—*
MUHAMMAD ABD AL-SALAM FARAJ

1. John Calvert, *Sayyid Qutb and the Origins of Radical Islamism* (New York: Columbia University Press, 2010), p. 282.

2. On the Society of Muslims, see Gilles Kepel, *The Roots of Radical Islam* (London: Saqi Books, 2005), chap. 3.

3. Kepel, *Roots of Radical Islam*, chap. 7; Johannes J. G. Jansen, *The Neglected Duty: The Creed of Sadat's Assassins* (New York: RVP, 2013), chap. 1.

4. Muhammad Abd al-Salam Faraj, "The Neglected Duty," §49, in Jansen, *Neglected Duty*. *The Neglected Duty* is organized not by chapters but by sections or perhaps stanzas.

5. Faraj, "Neglected Duty," §100.

6. Ibid., §3.

7. Ibid., §4, 5, 6.

8. Ibid., §88, 89.

9. Ibid., §90.

10. Ibid., §50.

11. Ibid., §12.

12. Ibid., §17.

13. Ibid., §18.

14. Ibid., §21–22.

15. Ibid., §25.

16. Ibid., §35.

17. Ibid., §20.

18. Ibid., §6.

19. Ibid., §83.

20. Ibid., §60–62.

21. Ibid., §81.

22. Ibid., §48–64.
23. Ibid., §84–87.
24. Ibid., §66.
25. Ibid., §92–93.
26. Ibid., §92–93.
27. Ibid., §99.
28. Ibid., §107.
29. Ibid., §109.
30. Ibid., §123–25.
31. Ibid., §71–80.
32. Ibid., §113.
33. Ibid., §122.
34. Ibid., §91.
35. Kepel, *Roots of Radical Islam*, pp. 217–25.
36. Faraj, "Neglected Duty," §68–70.
37. Ibid., §130–40.
38. For an overview, see Gilles Kepel, *Jihad: The Trail of Political Islam* (London and New York: I. B. Tauris, 2008), chap. 12.
39. Lawrence Wright, *The Looming Tower: Al-Qaeda's Road to 9/11* (New York: Penguin, 2006), pp. 259–61.
40. John C. Zimmerman, "Sayyid Qutb's Influence on the September 11 Attacks," *Terrorism and Political Violence* 16, no. 2 (2010): 223.
41. Faraj, "Neglected Duty," §27.
42. Ibid., §31.
43. Ibid., §10–11.
44. James Toth, *Sayyid Qutb: The Life and Legacy of a Radical Islamic Intellectual* (New York: Oxford University Press, 2013), p. 114.

CHAPTER 4: *JOIN THE CARAVAN*— ABDULLAH AZZAM

1. For details of Azzam's life, see Muhammad Haniff Hassan, *Father of Jihad: 'Abd Allah 'Azza m's Jihad Ideas and Implications to National Security* (London: Imperial College Press, 2014); Bernard Rougier, *Everyday Jihad: The Rise of Militant Islam among Palestinians in Lebanon,* trans. Pascale Ghazaleh (Cambridge, MA: Harvard University Press, 2007), chap. 2; Thomas Hegghammer, "Abdallah Azzam and Palestine," *Welt des Islams,* 53-3-4 (2013): 353–87; Andrew McGregor, "'Jihad and Rifle Alone': Abdullah Azzam and the Islamist Revolution," *Journal of Conflict Studies* 23, no. 2 (2003).

2. Mustafa Hamid and Leah Farrall, *The Arabs at War in Afghanistan* (London: Hurst, 2015), *passim*; Lawrence Wright, *The Looming Tower: Al-Qaeda's Road to 9/11* (New York: Penguin, 2006), chaps. 5–6; Rougier, *Everyday Jihad,* chap. 2.

3. Abdullah Azzam, *Join the Caravan,* translator's foreword, accessed at Religioscope online.

4. Hegghammer, "Abdallah Azzam and Palestine."

5. Hamid and Farrall, *Arabs at War in Afghanistan,* p. 124.

6. There are several online versions. The one I have consulted is Abdullah Azzam, *The Signs of Ar-Rahmaan in the Jihad of Afghanistan* (*Miracles of Jihad*), ed. A. B. al-Mehri (Birmingham, England: Maktabah Booksellers and Publishers, n.d.), www.maktabah.net.

7. Azzam, *Miracles of Jihad,* pp. 32–56.

8. Ibid., p. 31.

9. Frances L. Flannery, *Understanding Apocalyptic Terrorism* (Abingdon and New York: Routledge, 2015), p. 97.

10. This section is based on Azzam, *Miracles of Jihad*, "Conclusions," pp. 60–80.

11. Azzam, *Join the Caravan*, pt. 3, p. 3.

12. Abdullah Azzam, *The Defence of the Muslim Lands*, chap. 2, p. 4, accessed at Religioscope online.

13. Thomas Hegghammer, "The Rise of Muslim Foreign Fighters: Islam and the Globalization of Jihad," *International Security* 35, no. 3 (Winter 2010/2011): 53–94.

14. Hamid and Farrall, *Arabs at War in Afghanistan*, p. 310.

15. Azzam, *Join the Caravan*, pt. 1, p. 3.

16. Azzam, *Defence of the Muslim Lands*, chap. 4, p. 6.

17. Azzam, *Join the Caravan*, pt. 3, pp. 3–4.

18. Azzam, *Defence of the Muslim Lands*, chap. 4, p. 6.

19. Nelly Lahoud, *Jihadis' Path to Self-Destruction* (New York: Columbia University Press, 2010), p. 227.

20. The best study of Azzam's thought is Hassan, *Father of Jihad*. See also John C. M. Calvert, "The Striving Shaykh: Abdullah Azzam and the Revival of Jihad," *Journal of Religion and Society*, Supplement Series 2 (2007): 83–102.

21. Azzam, *Join the Caravan*, pt. 1, p. 1.

22. Hassan al-Banna, *The Complete Works of Imam Hasan al-Banna, 1906–1949*, no. 10, "al-Jihad."

23. Azzam, *Defence of the Muslim Lands*, chap. 1, p. 2; chap. 3, p. 1.

24. Ibid., chap. 1, p. 3.

25. Azzam, *Join the Caravan*, pt. 1, p. 7.

26. Azzam, *Defence of the Muslim Lands*, chap. 3, p. 3.

27. Azzam, *Join the Caravan*, pt. 1, p. 5.

28. Ibid., pt. 3, pp. 1–5.

29. Azzam, *Defence of the Muslim Lands*, chap. 4, pp. 3–4.

30. Ibid., chap. 1, p. 6.

31. Ibid., chap. 3, p. 4.

32. Ibid., chap. 2, pp. 1–2.

33. Ibid., chap. 4, pp. 6–8.

34. Ibid., chap. 4, pp. 8–10.

35. Ibid., chap. 4, p. 10.

36. Ibid., chap. 2, p. 1.

37. Azzam, *Join the Caravan*, pt. 2, p. 5.

38. Azzam, *Defence of the Muslim Lands*, chap. 3, p. 3.

39. Ibid., chap. 3, p. 1.

40. Azzam, *Join the Caravan*, pt. 2, p. 1.

41. Azzam, *Defence of the Muslim Lands*, chap. 3, p. 2.

42. Ibid., chap. 3, pp. 1–2.

43. Azzam, *Join the Caravan*, pt. 2, p. 1.

44. Ibid., pt. 1, p. 9.

45. Ibid., pt. 1, p. 1

46. Hassan, *Father of Jihad*, p. 19; Azzam, *Join the Caravan*, pt. 1, p. 15.

47. Azzam, *Join the Caravan*, pt. 1, p. 11.

48. Abdullah Azzam, *Martyrs: The Building Blocks of Nations*, accessed at Religioscope online.

49. This section is based on Hassan, *Father of Jihad*, esp. chap. 3.

50. Ibid., p. 175.

51. Ibid., p. 141.

52. Hegghammer, "Rise of Muslim Foreign Fighters."

53. Azzam, *Defence of the Muslim Lands*, chap. 4, p. 3.

54. Bruce Lawrence, ed., *Messages to the World: The Statements of Osama bin Laden* (London and New York: Verso, 2005), p. 77.

55. Rougier, *Everyday Jihad*, p. 83; the most interesting account is Mustafa Hamid's "Reflections," in Hamid and Farrall, *Arabs at War in Afghanistan*, pp. 293–325.

56. Hassan, *Father of Jihad*, p. 175.

57. Hamid and Farrall, *Arabs at War in Afghanistan, passim*.

CHAPTER 5: *KNIGHTS UNDER THE PROPHET'S BANNER—* OSAMA BIN LADEN AND AYMAN AL-ZWAHIRI

1. Fawaz A. Gerges, *The Far Enemy: Why Jihad Went Global* (New York: Cambridge University Press, 2009), chap. 3.

2. Abdullah Azzam, *The Defence of the Muslim Lands*, intro., p. 2, accessed at Religioscope online.

3. Lawrence Wright, *The Looming Tower: Al-Qaeda's Road to 9/11* (New York: Penguin, 2006), chaps. 5–7; Mustafa Hamid and Leah Farrall, *Arabs at War in Afghanistan* (London: Hurst, 2015), pp. 313–22.

4. Wright, *Looming Tower*, pp. 154–58; Gerges, *Far Enemy*, pp. 145–50.

5. Wright, *Looming Tower*, chaps. 8–13; Hamid and Farrall, *Arabs at War in Afghanistan*, chap. 9; Bruce Lawrence, ed., *Messages to the World: The Statements of Osama bin Laden* (London and New York: Verso, 2005), p. 26.

6. Lawrence, *Messages to the World*, pp. 1–57.

7. Ibid., pp. 23–30.

8. Ibid., pp. 46–48.

9. Ibid., pp. 58–62.

10. Gerges, *Far Enemy*, p. 118.

11. Hamid and Farrall, *Arabs at War in Afghanistan*, pp. 211–13.

12. Gerges, *Far Enemy*, p. 33.

13. Ibid., chap. 4; Hamid and Farrall, *Arabs at War in Afghanistan*, pp. 278–81.

14. Lawrence, *Messages to the World*, p. 40.

15. Steven Brooke, "Jihadist Strategic Debates before 9/11," *Studies in Conflict & Terrorism* 31 (2008): 201–26.

16. Zawahiri has provided a firsthand account of these operations in *Knights under the Prophet's Banner*, in *His Own Words: A Translation of the Writings of Dr. Ayman al Zawahiri*, ed. Laura Mansfield(Old Tappan, NJ: TLG Publications, 2006), pp. 95–108; see also Steven Brooke, "Jihadist Strategic Debates before 9/11," *Studies in Conflict & Terrorism* 31, no. 3 (2008): 209–12; Assaf Moghadam, *The Globalization of Martyrdom: Al Qaeda, Salafi Jihad and the Diffusion of Suicide Attacks* (Baltimore, MD: Johns Hopkins University Press, 2008), chap. 2; Gilles Kepel, *Jihad: The Trail of Political Islam* (London and New York: I. B. Tauris, 2008), chap. 12.

17. The treatise, given the new title, "Jihad, Martyrdom, and the Killing of Innocents," is published unabridged in *The Al Qaeda Reader: The Essential Texts of Osama bin Laden's Terrorist Organization*, ed. Raymond Ibrahim (New York: Broadway Books, 2007), pp. 137–71.

18. Moghadam, *Globalization of Martyrdom*, p. 251.

19. Michael Kraft and Edward Marks, *U.S. Government Counterterrorism* (Boca Raton, FL: CRC, 2016), p. 286.

20. Zawahiri, *Knights*, p. 58.

21. Ibid., pp. 22–42.

22. Ibid., pp. 47–50.

23. Ibid., pp. 72 and 170–74.

24. Nimrod Raphaeli, "Ayman al-Zawahiri," Jewish Virtual Library, 2002, p. 2.

25. Zawahiri, *Knights*, p. 73.

26. Ibid., p. 74.

27. Ibid., pp. 111–19.

28. Ibid., pp. 160–69.

29. Ibid., pp. 137–60.

30. Ibid., pp. 176–200.

31. Ibid., p. 205.

32. Ibid., esp. pp. 200 and 212.

33. Ibid., pp. 219–20.

34. Ibid., pp. 222–23.

35. Ibid., p. 225.

36. Ibid., p. 115.

CHAPTER 6: *THE MANAGEMENT OF SAVAGERY—* ABU BAKR NAJI AND ABU MUS'AB AL-ZARQAWI

1. Mustafa Hamid and Leah Farrall, *The Arabs at War in Afghanistan* (London: Hurst, 2015), *passim.*

2. This section is based on Bruce Lawrence, ed., *Messages to the World: The Statements of Osama bin Laden* (London and New York: Verso, 2005), pts. 4 and 5.

3. Malcolm Nance, *Defeating ISIS: Who They Are, How They Fight, What They Believe* (New York: Skyhorse Publishing, 2016), p. 303.

4. William McCants, *The ISIS Apocalypse: The History, Strategy and Doomsday Vision of the Islamic State* (New York: St. Martin's, 2015), p. 84.

5. Abu Bakr Naji, *The Management of Savagery,* trans. John B. Hardie (New York: Islamic Publications International, 200), p. 7. Note: The McCants translation uses only the page numbers of the original Arabic version.

6. Ibid., pp. 7–8.

7. Ibid., pp. 9–10.

8. Ibid., p. 92.

9. Ibid., p. 76.

10. Ibid., p. 44.

11. Ibid., p. 15.

12. Ibid., p. 14.

13. Ibid., p. 61.

14. Ibid., p. 37.

15. Ibid., pp. 37–39.

16. Ibid., p. 19.

17. Ibid., p., 46.

18. Ibid., pp. 40–44.

19. Ibid., p. 30.

20. Ibid., pp. 66–67.

21. Ibid., p. 68.

22. Ibid., p. 32.

23. Ibid., p. 34.

24. Ibid., p. 32.

25. Ibid., p. 46.

26. Ibid., pp. 47 and 52.

27. Ibid., pp. 26–27.

28. Ibid., p. 52.

29. Ibid., p. 53.

30. Ibid., p. 31.

31. Ibid., p. 59.

32. Ibid., pp. 81–82.

33. Ibid., pp. 91–92.

34. Ibid., p. 74.

35. Ibid., pp. 56–58.

36. Ibid., p. 79.

37. Ibid., pp. 101–105.

38. This section is based on Loretta Napoleoni, *Insurgent Iraq: Al Zarqawi and the New Generation* (New York: Seven Stories, 2005); Jean-Charles Brisard and Damien Martinez, *Zarqawi: The New Face of al-Qaeda* (Cambridge, UK: Polity, 2005); Gerges, *ISIS: A History*, chap. 2; Hassan Abu Hanieh and Mohammad Abu Rumman, *The "Islamic State" Organization* (Jordan and Iraq: Friedrich Ebert Stiftung, 2015); Mustafa Hamid and Leah Farrall, *The Arabs at War in Afghanistan* (London: Hurst, 2015); Nimrod Raphaeli, "The Sheikh of the Slaughterers," Frontpage.com, July 6, 2005.

39. Michael Weiss and Hassan Hassan, *ISIS: Inside the Army of Terror* (New York: Regan Arts, 2015), p. 41.

40. "From Hijrah to Khalifah," *Dabiq*, no. 1.

41. Joas Wagemakers, *A Quietist Jihadi: The Ideology and Influence of Abu Muhammad al-Maqdisi* (New York: Cambridge University Press, 2012); Nibras Kazimi, "A Virulent Ideology in Mutation: Zarqawi Upstages Maqdisi," *Current Trends in Islamist Ideology* 2 (2005); Hanieh and Rumman, *"Islamic State" Organization*, pp. 80–82.

42. Abu Mus'ab al-Zarqawi, "Zarqawi Clarifies Issues Raised by Sheikh Maqdisi," July 21, 2005.

43. Hanieh and Rumman, *"Islamic State" Organization*, pp. 36–38.

44. Ibid., pp. 242–46.

45. Zarqawi's letter is published unabridged in Brisard, *Zarqawi*, pp. 233–51.

46. Hanieh and Rumman, *"Islamic State" Organization*, pp. 48–51; Gerges, *ISIS: A History*, pp. 72–81.

47. Zawahiri's letter is published unabridged in Laura Mansfield, ed., *His Own Words: A Translation of the Writings of Dr. Ayman al Zawahiri* (Old Tappan, NJ: TLG Publications, 2006), pp. 250–79.

48. Abu Mus'ab al-Zarqawi, "Leader of Al-Qaeda in Iraq al-Zarqawi Declares 'Total War' on Shi'ites," audiotape, September 16, 2005.

49. Al-Libi's letter can be found at Combating Terrorism Center, www.ctc.usma.edu/harmony/CTC-AtiyahLetter.pdf.

50. Bernard Haykel, "Al-Qa'ida and Shiism," in *Fault Lines in Global Jihad*, ed. Assaf Moghadam and Brian Fishman (London: Routledge, 2011), pp. 184–202; Nibras Kazimi, "Zarqawi's Anti-Shi'a Legacy: Original or Borrowed?" *Current Trends in Islamist Ideology* 4 (2006).

51. Zarqawi, "Zarqawi Clarifies Issues."

52. Haykel, "Al-Qa'ida and Shiism."

53. The creed is published by Bernard Haykel as an appendix to his chapter, "On the Nature of Salafi Thought and Action," in *Global Salafism: Islam's New Religious Movement*, ed. Roel Meijer (London: Hurst, 2009).

54. Haykel, "Al Qa'ida and Shiism," p. 189.

55. Abu Omar al-Baghdadi, "Abu-Umar al-Baghdadi Views 'Dividends and Losses' after Four Years of 'Jihad,'" audio transcript, April 17, 2007.

56. Martha L. Cottam and Joe W. Huseby, *Confronting Al Qaeda: The Sunni Awakening and American Strategy in Al Anbar* (London: Rowman and Littlefield, 2016), p. 71.

57. McCants, *ISIS Apocalypse*, p. 42.

CHAPTER 7: *DABIQ:* THE MIND OF THE ISLAMIC STATE

1. Translation of Ayman al-Zawahiri's letter to the two jihadi groups can be found at "Translation of al-Qaeda Chief Ayman al-Zawahiri's Letter to the Leaders of the Two Jihadi Groups," http://s3.documentcloud.org/documents/710588/translation-of-ayman-al-zawahiris-letter.pdf.

2. Analyses of these years can be found in Fawaz A. Gerges, *ISIS: A History* (Princeton and Oxford: Princeton University Press, 2016); Hassan Abu Hanieh and Mohammad Abu Rumman, *The "Islamic State" Organization* (Jordan and Iraq: Friedrich Ebert Stiftung, 2015); William McCants, *The ISIS Apocalypse: The History, Strategy, and Doomsday Vision of the Islamic State* (New York: St. Martin's, 2015), chap. 4.

3. Ayman al-Zawahiri, *General Guidelines for Jihad*, 2013.

4. Hanieh and Rumman, *"Islamic State" Organization*, pp. 198–203.

5. Gerges, *ISIS: A History*, pp. 187–201.

6. There is a little information about *Dabiq* in Hanieh and Rumman, *"Islamic State" Organization*, pp. 274–75.

7. "From Hijrah to Khalifah," *Dabiq*, no. 1.

8. "Interview with Abu Muqatil," *Dabiq*, no. 8, p. 60.

9. "James Wright Foley," *Dabiq*, no. 3, p. 4.

10. "A Message from Sotloff to His Mother," *Dabiq*, no. 4, pp. 47–51.

11. "Foreword," *Dabiq*, no. 7, pp. 3–4.

12. Excerpts from "Indeed Your Lord Is Ever Watchful," *Dabiq*, no. 4, p. 9.

13. "I used to be a Rafidi, but not anymore. Now I am a Muslim." "Foreword," *Dabiq*, no. 6, pp. 3–5.

14. "Islamic State Operations," *Dabiq*, no. 15, p. 43.

15. "Foreword," *Dabiq*, no. 12, pp. 2–3. The cover is entitled "Just Terror."

16. "The Capture of a Crusader Pilot," *Dabiq*, no. 6, pp. 34–37.

17. "The Burning of the Murtadd Pilot," *Dabiq*, no. 7, pp. 5–8.

18. Among the many examples: "Execution of Nusrayi Soldiers," *Dabiq*, no. 3, p. 21; "The Humiliated Followers of the Coptic Church," *Dabiq*, no. 7, p. 32.

19. "Harvesting the Sahwah," *Dabiq*, no. 9, p. 28.

20. McCants, *ISIS Apocalypse*, pp. 145–46.

21. "The Liberation of Dabiq," *Dabiq*, no. 3, p. 15; see also McCants, *ISIS Apocalypse*, pp. 102–105.

22. *Dabiq*, no. 4, p. 35.

23. "You will have a treaty of security with the Romans until you both fight an enemy beyond them." "Reflections on the Final Crusade," *Dabiq*, no. 4, p. 33; John Cantlie, "Paradigm Shift," *Dabiq*, no. 8, pp. 64–67.

24. "The Revival of Slavery before the Hour," *Dabiq*, no. 4, pp. 14–17.

25. "Slave Girls or Prostitutes?" *Dabiq*, no. 9, p. 49.

26. For example, *Dabiq*, no. 13, pp. 41–42.

27. "The 'Mahdi' of the Rafidah: The Dajjal," *Dabiq*, no. 11, pp. 16–17.

28. The most detailed account of the evil of the Rafidah, where these words are found, is "The Rafidah: From Ibn Saba' to the Dajjal," *Dabiq*, no. 13, pp. 32–45.

29. "The Revival of Slavery before the Hour," *Dabiq*, no. 4, pp. 14–17.

30. "The Allies of Al-Qa'idah in Sham: Part III," *Dabiq*, no. 10, pp. 6–13.

31. "Dismantling a Khariji Cell," *Dabiq*, no. 6, p. 31.

32. "The Qa'ida of Adh-Dhawiri, Al-Harari, and An-Nadhari, and the Absent Yemeni Wisdom," *Dabiq*, no. 6, pp. 16–25; "Al-Qa'ida of Waziristan," *Dabiq*, no. 6, pp. 40–55.

33. "Revenge for the Muslimāt Persecuted by the Coptic Crusaders of Egypt," *Dabiq*, no. 7, p. 32; "Soldiers of Terror," *Dabiq*, no. 8, p. 19; "Interview with Abu Muharib," *Dabiq*, no. 12, pp. 59–62; "The Murtadd Brotherhood," *Dabiq*, no. 14, p. 30.

34. *Dabiq*, no. 13, p. 42.

35. The regular *Dabiq* feature on the martyrs is called "Among the Believers Are Men."

36. "You Think They Are Together, But Their Hearts Are Divided," *Dabiq*, no. 12, p. 46.

37. "By the Sword," *Dabiq*, no. 15, p. 80. The article is completed with a photo of a gruesome beheading, captioned: "The sword is part of Allah's law."

BIBLIOGRAPHY

PRIMARY SOURCES

Dabiq, 2014–2016, nos. 1–15.

David Aaron (ed.), 2008, *In Their Own Words: Voices of Jihad*, RAND Corporation, Santa Monica.

Abdullah Azzam, n.d., *The Defence of the Muslim Lands*, accessed at Religioscope online.

———, n.d., *Join the Caravan*, accessed at Religioscope online.

———, n.d., *Martyrs: The Building Blocks of Nations*, accessed at Religioscope online.

———, n.d., *The Signs of Ar-Rahmaan in the Jihad of Afghanistan*, edited by A. B. al-Mehri, Maktabah Booksellers and Publishers, Birmingham, England.

Abu Omar al-Baghdadi, "Abu-Umar al-Baghdadi Views 'Dividends and Losses' after Four Years of 'Jihad,'" audio transcript, April 17, 2007.

Hassan al-Banna, *The Complete Works of Imam Hasan al-Banna, 1906–1949*, nos. 1–10.

Albert J. Bergsten (ed.), 2008, *The Sayyid Qutb Reader: Selected Writings on Politics, Religion and Society*, Routledge, New York.

Muhammad Abd al-Salam Faraj, 2013, "The Neglected Duty," in Johannes J. G. Jansen, *The Neglected Duty: The Creed of Sadat's Assassins*, RVP Press, New York.

Raymond Ibrahim (ed.), 2007, *The Al Qaeda Reader: The*

Essential Texts of Osama bin Laden's Terrorist Organization, Broadway Books, New York.

Gilles Kepel and Jean-Pierre Milelli (eds.), 2008, *Al Qaeda in its Own Words,* Belknap Press, Cambridge, Massachusetts.

Bruce Lawrence (ed.), 2005, *Messages to the World: The Statements of Osama bin Laden,* Verso, London and New York.

Atiyatullah al-Libi, Letter to al-Zarqawi, www.ctc.usma.edu/harmony/CTC-AtiyahLetter.pdf.

Laura Mansfield (ed.), 2006, *His Own Words: A Translation of the Writings of Dr. Ayman al Zawahiri,* TLG Publications, Old Tappan, NJ.

Sayyid Abul A'la Maududi, 1998, *Our Message,* Islamic Publications, Lahore.

Abu Bakr Naji, 2006, *The Management of Savagery,* translated by William McCants for the John M. Olin Institute for Strategic Studies, Harvard University.

Sayyid Qutb, 2000, *Social Justice in Islam,* translated by John B. Hardie, Islamic Publications International, New York.

———, 2005, *Milestones,* Islamic Book Service, New Delhi, reprint edition.

Abu Mus'ab al-Zarqawi, ca. January 2004, "Letter to Al Qaeda Central," Appendix VIII in Jean-Charles Brisard with Damien Martinez, 2005, *Zarqawi: The New Face of al-Qaeda,* Polity Press, Cambridge, UK.

———, July 21, 2005, "Zarqawi Clarifies Issues Raised by Sheikh Maqdisi."

———, September 16, 2005, "Leader of Al-Qaeda in Iraq Al-Zarqawi Declares 'Total War' on Shi'ites."

Ayman al-Zawahiri, 2013, *General Guidelines for Jihad.*

———, n.d., Translation of al-Qaeda chief Ayman

al-Zawahiri's letter to the two jihadi groups, http://
s3.documentcloud.org/documents/710588/translation-of-
ayman-al-zawahiris-letter.pdf.

SECONDARY SOURCES

"Abu Mus'ab al Zarqawi under Influence: One Mentor?" n.d.,
Alleyesonjihadism blog.

"Battle for Fallujah: Mass Grave with 400 Bodies Found in
Iraq," June 6, 2016, *Sydney Morning Herald.*

Peter Bergen and Paul Cruickshank, 2012, "Revisiting the
Early Al Qaeda: An Updated Account of its Formative
Years," *Studies in Conflict & Terrorism*, vol. 35, no. 1.

Mohamed Bin Ali, 2014, *The Roots of Religious Extremism:
Understanding the Salafi Doctrine of Al-Wala' wal Bara,"*
Imperial College Press, London.

Alia Brahimi, 2009, "Crushed in the Shadows: Why Al Qaeda
Will Lose the War of Ideas," *Studies in Conflict & Terrorism*,
vol. 33, no. 2.

Jean-Charles Brisard and Damien Martinez, 2005, *Zarqawi: The
New Face of al-Qaeda*, Polity Press, Cambridge, UK.

Steven Brooke, 2008, "Jihadist Strategic Debates before 9/11,"
Studies in Conflict & Terrorism, vol. 31, no. 3.

Cole Bunzel, March 2015, "From Paper State to Caliphate:
The Ideology of the Islamic State," The Brookings Project
on U.S. Relations with the Islamic World, Analysis Paper,
no. 19.

Jason Burke, 2007, *Al-Qaeda: The True Story of Radical Islam*,
Penguin, London.

John Calvert, 2007, "The Striving Shaykh: Abdullah Azzam and the Revival of Jihad," *Journal of Religion and Society*, Supplement Series 2 (edited by Ronald A. Simkins).

———, 2010, *Sayyid Qutb and the Origins of Radical Islamism*, Columbia University Press, New York.

Patrick Cockburn, 2015, *The Rise of the Islamic State: ISIS and the New Sunni Revolution*, Verso, London.

Martha L. Cottam and Joe W. Huseby, 2016, *Confronting Al Qaeda: The Sunni Awakening and American Strategy in al Anbar*, Rowman & Littlefield, London.

Robyn Creswell and Bernard Haykel, June 8 and 15, 2015, "Battle Lines: Want to Understand the Jihadis? Read Their Poetry," *New Yorker*.

Michael Cromartie, with Bernard Haykel and William McCants, 2015, "The Islamic State: Understanding its Ideology and Theology," Speech at the May 2015 Faith Angle Forum.

Lawrence Davidson, 2013, *Islamic Fundamentalism*, 3rd edition, Praeger, Santa Barbara.

Emmen El-Badawy, Milo Comerford, and Peter Welby, 2015, *Inside the Jihadi Mind: Understanding Ideology and Propaganda*, Center on Religion & Geopolitics, Tony Blair Faith Foundation.

Frances L. Flannery, 2015, *Understanding Apocalyptic Terrorism: Countering the Radical Mindset*, Routledge, Abingdon and New York.

Fawaz A. Gerges, 2009, *The Far Enemy: Why Jihad Went Global*, Cambridge University Press, New York.

———, 2016, *ISIS: A History*, Princeton University Press, Princeton and Oxford.

John Gray, July 27, 2002, "How Marx Turned Muslim,"
Independent.

Mustafa Hamid and Leah Farrall, 2015, *The Arabs at War in Afghanistan*, Hurst & Company, London.

Hassan Abu Hanieh and Mohammad Abu Rumman, 2015, *The "Islamic State" Organization*, Friedrich Ebert Stiftung, Jordan and Iraq.

Hassan Hassan, June 13, 2016, "The Sectarianism of the Islamic State: Ideological Roots and Political Context," Carnegie Endowment for International Peace.

Muhammad Haniff Hassan, 2014, *The Father of Jihad: 'Abd Allah 'Azzām's Jihad Ideas and Implications to National Security*, Imperial College Press, London.

Bernard Haykel, 2011, "Al-Qa'ida and Shiism," in Assaf Moghadam and Brian Fishman (eds.), *Fault Lines in Global Jihad*, Routledge, London.

———, 2009, "On the Nature of Salafi Thought and Action," in Roel Meijer (ed.), 2009, *Global Salafism: Islam's New Religious Movement*, Hurst & Company, London.

Thomas Hegghammer, 2010/11, "The Rise of Muslim Foreign Fighters: Islam and the Globalization of Jihad," *International Security*, vol. 35, no. 3 (Winter).

———, 2013, "Abdallah Azzam and Palestine," *Welt des Islams* 53-3-4.

Christopher Hitchens, October 22, 2007, "Defending Islamofascism," *Slate.*

Roy Jackson, 2010, *Mawlana Mawdudi and Political Islam: Authority and the Islamic State*, Routledge, London and New York.

Johannes J. G. Jansen, 2002, "Faraj and the Neglected Duty," *Interview*, Religioscope.

————, 2013, *The Neglected Duty: The Creed of Sadat's Assassins*, RVP Press, New York.

Nibras Kazimi, 2005, "A Virulent Ideology in Mutation: Zarqawi Upstages Maqdisi," *Current Trends in Islamist Ideology*, vol. 2.

————, 2006, "Zarqawi's Anti-Shi'a Legacy: Original or Borrowed?" *Current Trends in Islamist Ideology*, vol. 4.

Gilles Kepel, 2005, *The Roots of Radical Islam*, Saqi Books, London.

————, 2008, *Jihad: The Trail of Political Islam*, I. B. Tauris, London and New York.

Sayed Khatab, 2006, *The Political Thought of Sayyid Qutb: The Theory of Jahiliyyah*, Routledge, Abingdon.

David Kilcullen, 2016, *Blood Year: Islamic State and the Failures of the War on Terror*, Black Inc., Melbourne.

Michael Kraft and Edward Marks, 2016, *U.S. Government Counterterrorism*, CRC Press, Boca Raton, Florida.

Nelly Lahoud, 2010, *The Jihadis' Path to Self-Destruction*, Columbia University Press, New York.

Bruce Lawrence (ed.), 2005, *Messages to the World: The Statements of Osama bin Laden*, Verso, London and New York.

Brynjar Lia, 2014, *Architect of Global Jihad: The Life of Al-Qaeda Strategist Abu Mus'ab Al-Suri*, Hurst & Company, London.

Mark Lynch, 2010, "Islam Divided between Salafi-Jihad and the Ikhwan," *Studies in Conflict & Terrorism*, vol. 33.

Shiraz Maher, 2016, *Salafi-Jihadism: The History of an Idea*, Oxford University Press, New York.

Shiv Malik, Ali Younes, Spencer Ackerman, and Mustafa Khalil, December 19, 2014, "The Race to Save Peter Kassig," *Guardian*.

Robert Manne, 2003, "Explaining the Invasion," in Raimond
  Gaita (ed.), *Why the War Was Wrong*, Text Publishing,
  Melbourne.
William McCants, 2015, *The ISIS Apocalypse: The History, Strategy,
  and Doomsday Vision of the Islamic State*, St. Martin's, New York.
Andrew McGregor, 2003, "'Jihad and Rifle Alone': "Abdullah
  Azzam and the Islamist Revolution," *Journal of Conflict
  Studies*, vol. 23, no. 2.
Roel Meijer (ed.), 2009, *Global Salafism: Islam's New Religious
  Movement*, Hurst & Company, London.
Richard P. Mitchell, 1969, *The Society of the Muslim Brothers*,
  Oxford University Press, London.
Assaf Moghadam, 2008, *The Globalization of Martyrdom: Al
  Qaeda, Salafi Jihad and the Diffusion of Suicide Attacks*, Johns
  Hopkins University Press, Baltimore.
Assaf Moghadam and Brian Fishman (eds.), 2011, *Fault Lines
  in Global Jihad*, Routledge, London.
Adnan A. Musallam, 2005, *From Secularism to Jihad*, Praeger,
  Westport, Connecticut.
Malcolm Nance, 2016, *Defeating ISIS: Who They Are, How They
  Fight, What They Believe*, Skyhorse Publishing, New York.
Loretta Napoleoni, 2005, *Insurgent Iraq: Al Zarqawi and the New
  Generation*, Seven Stories Press, New York.
Nimrod Raphaeli, 2002, "Ayman al-Zawahiri," Jewish Virtual
  Library.
————, July 6, 2005, "The Sheikh of the Slaughterers,"
  Frontpagemag.com.
David Remnick, January 27, 2014, "Going the Distance," *New
  Yorker*.
Bernard Rougier, 2007, *Everyday Jihad: The Rise of Militant*

Islam among Palestinians in Lebanon, translated by
Pascale Ghazaleh, Harvard University Press, Cambridge,
Massachusetts.

Olivier Roy, 2004, *Globalized Islam: The Search for the New
Ummah,* Hurst & Company, London.

Erin Marie Saltman and Charlie Winter, 2014, *Islamic State:
The Changing Face of Modern Jihadism,* Quilliam Foundation.

William E. Shepard, 2003, "Sayyid Qutb's Doctrine of Jahiliyya,"
International Journal of Middle Eastern Studies, vol. 35.

Jessica Stern and J. M. Berger, 2015, *ISIS: The State of Terror,*
William Collins, London.

James Toth, 2013, *Sayyid Qutb: The Life and Legacy of a Radical
Islamic Intellectual,* Oxford University Press, New York.

Joas Wagemakers, 2012, *A Quietist Jihadi: The Ideology and
Influence of Abu Muhammad al-Maqdisi,* Cambridge
University Press, New York.

Michael Weiss and Hassan Hassan, 2015, *ISIS: Inside the Army of
Terror,* Regan Arts, New York.

Quintan Wiktorowicz, 2001, "Centrifugal Tendencies in the
Algerian Civil War," *Arab Studies Quarterly,* vol. 23, no. 3
(Summer).

———, 2005, "A Genealogy of Radical Islam," *Studies in
Conflict & Terrorism,* vol. 28.

———, 2006, "Anatomy of the Salafi Movement," *Studies in
Conflict & Terrorism,* vol. 29.

Quintan Wiktorowicz and John Kaltner, 2003, "Killing in the
Name of Islam: Al-Qaeda's Justification for September 11,"
Middle East Policy, vol. 10, no. 2 (Summer).

Graeme Wood, March 2015, "What ISIS Really Wants,"
Atlantic.

———, 2017, *The Way of the Strangers: Encounters with the Islamic State*, Penguin Random House, London.

Lawrence Wright, 2006, *The Looming Tower: Al-Qaeda's Road to 9/11*, Penguin, New York.

———, September 11, 2006, "The Master Plan: For the New Theorists of Jihad, Al Qaeda Is Just the Beginning," *New Yorker*.

John C. Zimmerman, 2010, "Sayyid Qutb's Influence on the September 11 Attacks," *Terrorism and Political Violence*, vol. 16, no. 2.